Y0-BQT-385

WITHDRAWN

LIBRARY
College of St. Scholastica
Duluth, Minnesota 55811

WITHDRAWN

USING
THE COMPUTER
IN THE
SOCIAL SCIENCES

USING
THE COMPUTER
IN THE
SOCIAL SCIENCES
A
Nontechnical Approach

Ronn J. Hy
Department of Political Science
The University of Mississippi

ELSEVIER
NEW YORK   OXFORD   AMSTERDAM

H
61
.H95

Elsevier North-Holland, Inc.
52 Vanderbilt Avenue, New York, New York 10017

Elsevier Scientific Publishing Company
335 Jan Van Galenstraat, P.O. Box 211
Amsterdam, The Netherlands

© 1977 by Elsevier North-Holland, Inc.

Library of Congress Cataloging in Publication Data
Hy, Ronn.
  Using the computer in the social sciences:
  a nontechnical approach
  Bibliography: p.
  Includes index.
  1. Social sciences — Data processing. 2. Elec-
  tronic data processing. 3. Report writing.
  I. Title.
H61.H95   300'.28'54   77-956
ISBN 0-444-00211-1
ISBN 0-444-00220-0 pbk.

Manufactured in the United States of America.

To Star, Adeline, and John

LIBRARY
College of St. Scholastica
Duluth, Minnesota 55811

CONTENTS

Preface

2. Computer-oriented research has become so popular and valuable that it now is being taught in an inchoate form to freshman and sophomore social-science students. This trend has resulted in a plethora of books designed to help students learn about the research process. Most of these books, unfortunately, are too complex for beginners to comprehend. Thus, any person who has ever taught or taken a beginning research course can attest to the need for a short, simple book which dispels novices' fears about quantitative research by showing them, in terms peppered with concrete examples, how actually to use the computer to write a report. The objective of this volume, then, is to introduce the main components of a computer, the principal statistical packages used by social scientists, and some elementary

techniques employed in the writing of a research report. This knowledge, it is felt, is presented in a way that conveys to neophytes the idea that quantitative research is really not that difficult. Throughout this volume, the emphasis is on helping the reader understand and use the computer in order to write a research report. As a result, the book is broad enough to be used as a supplementary text for a wide variety of social-science courses, especially since it is assumed that the reader has no background in quantitative research.

At this juncture, two comments are in order. In the first place, the quotations that appear in the volume *must be read*, since they explain and define crucial concepts and terms. This caveat is stated explicitly because many readers often skim over quotations rather than ingest them as part of the text. Furthermore, the reader who has absolutely no background in research design or statistics probably should glance at Chapter 4 before tackling the entire book. This chapter provides the reader with an understanding of the research process; hence, he will have a better idea of why the other material presented in this volume is important as well as how the information will eventually be used.

Many persons have helped me prepare this book. Although it is impossible to cite each individually, a few deserve special thanks. I am particularly indebted to Mrs. Leonora Presley who stoically typed and retyped the manuscript; to Herbert Waltzer who provided me with the skills with which to write this volume; and to my students at the University of Mississippi whose blank stares and illuminated faces pointed me in the right direction. I also would like to thank the Bureau of Governmental Research and the Department of Political Science, which gave me time and assistance to complete this project. I gratefully acknowledge use of examples of machinery manufactured by International Business Machine Corporation (Figures 2.2, 2.3, A.1, and A.2) and Digital Equipment Corporation (Figures 2.4—2.11). Last, but by no means least, I wish to thank my wife Star, who helped me immensely.

Needless to say, all errors and omissions are mine.

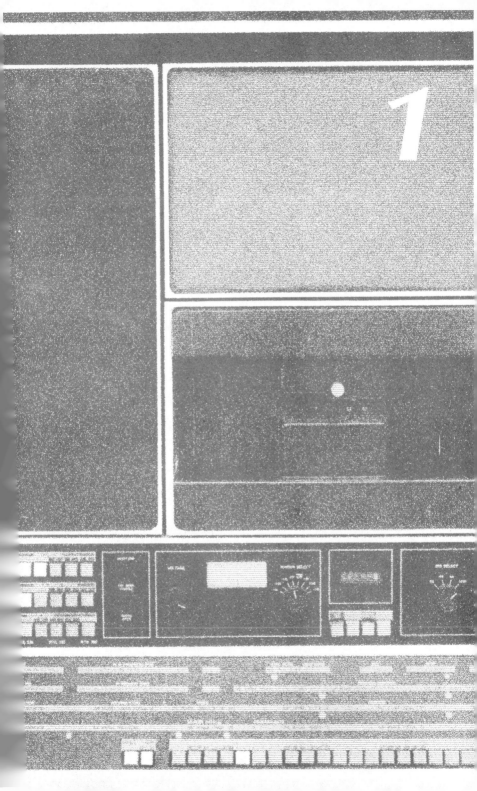

Introduction

Today, as never before, the digital electronic computer is of ever-increasing importance in the processing of data for social research because the computer makes it feasible to handle large quantities of data quickly, conveniently, and accurately. Tabulations which without the computer would take days, and even weeks, can be carried out in a matter of minutes with it. This capability is significant because in recent years tremendous emphasis has been placed on studying quantifiable social behavior. This trend has led to the evolution and use of statistical and methodological techniques which are founded on the assumption that the larger the number of cases examined, the closer to reality the findings will be.

The only feasible way to process so many cases is with the

aid of a computer and its symbiotic statistical capabilities. For instance, to hand-manipulate and hand-calculate various relational statistics for data gathered from 2000 questionnaires is virtually impossible. With the aid of a computer, such data can be processed and varied statistics calculated in a matter of seconds with less computational error than if performed by an individual. Moreover, as the power of the machine increases with each new hardware and software development, the computer's capabilities expand, so that users can work with more complex and precise models which include larger slices of reality.

Peter Harkins and his associates have listed six predominant ways in which the computer lessens the mechanical aspects of a social scientist's workload, thus freeing him to concentrate on substantive facets of research—that is, the study and evaluation of complex and intricate interactions between and among individuals, societies, and institutions. These six ways are as follows:

1. Computers can routinely and conveniently perform numerical calculations more rapidly and accurately than if performed by hand. (A second generation computer of the IBM 7090 class can perform approximately the equivalent of a man-life of calculations every two hours. For third-generation computers this time is reduced to minutes.)
2. Computers can produce answers which would be useless if the time for hand calculations were required. (For example, the necessary calculations for correcting the trajectory of a spacecraft must frequently be accomplished within a limited time. By the time a hand calculation could be done the answer might be only academic.)
3. Certain types of problems may be optimized or simulated by computer calculations. (For example, redis-

tricting congressional delegations and reapportioning state houses and senates may be accomplished with a minimum of partisan political overtones through a computer simulation. The growth and development of metropolitan areas may be simulated decades into the future—a powerful tool for both planners and politicians.)

4. Computers are routinely used for information storage and the retrieval, organization, management, and presentation of large data banks. (For example, thousands of source documents may be searched for certain key words or concepts. The questions asked in a hundred or more surveys, along with a frequency distribution of their answers, may be catalogued in such a way that an investigator could access all questions bearing on "the cost of living" or "attitudes toward the Supreme Court".)

5. Computers can be used to gather data from experiments as these data are produced (in real time); and they can often be incorporated into experimental apparatus so that they direct the experiment as it actually takes place. (For example, intensive-care units in hospitals continuously monitor patient physiological signs by computer.)

6. Computers can be programmed to display intelligence by learning to perform tasks while improving their success as their experience increases. (Some advocates of machine intelligence go so far as to say that computers are essentially a new life form with nearly limitless possibilities.)[1]

Fortunately, a person need not understand the intricate internal operations of a computer in order to use it. But

[1]Peter B. Harkins et al., *Introduction to Computer Programming for the Social Sciences* (Boston: Allyn and Bacon, 1973), p. 4. Reprinted by permission of publisher.

when utilizing the machine, one should realize that he has a responsibility not to misuse it. In other words, investigators have to become knowledgeable enough to distinguish between erroneous uses and valid uses of the machine and its programs, for once a successful tool has been developed, there is always the danger that it will be overextended. Indeed, the proliferation of computer use has resulted in both the application and misapplication of various statistical techniques.

At this juncture, a word of caution needs to be stated explicitly. The statistically unsophisticated normally are overawed by quantitative analysis to the point that any such research is cited as fact. Needless to say, with this type of mental framework the possible misuses are limitless. As Stephen Campbell writes:

> So useful has the computer become in all branches of statistical analysis that there may be some tendency to forget that even it has its limitations. The computer cannot work magic—not yet anyway. It will do only what it is instructed to do, and the validity of the results is determined by the accuracy and adequacy of the data put in and the wisdom of the people writing the instructions. Granted, the computer can perform a great many calculations much more rapidly than mere mortals can do them. Nevertheless, speed of computational work is not the same thing as infallibility in aiding with the decision-making process. A statistical critic, of all people, should guard against being overawed by the news that certain information was turned out by a computer. The mere fact that computers are being used these days even to cast horoscopes should be ample proof that a computer is no more immune to spewing out nonsense than are real flesh-and-blood people.[2]

The investigator must never succumb to the temptation to believe that speed and accuracy are equal to infallibility.

[2]Stephen Campbell, *Flaws and Fallacies in Statistical Thinking* (Englewood Cliffs, N.J.: Prentice-Hall, 1974), p. 182. Reprinted by permission of publisher.

The validity of results is only as sound as the data and instructions fed into the machine. Computer output, in other words, must be scrutinized carefully with a combination of logic and common sense.

Then, too social researchers must realize the hazards involved in endeavoring to mimic physicists who write sets of differential equations for some physical process. By striving to identify the constants and parameters of a proposed theory, such investigators frequently use the computer, instead of logic, in an attempt to discover general laws. Stated another way, the computer often is abused by lazy minds venturing to find universal explanations or panaceas. Such elucidations, if they exist, are the product of the human mind and judgment, not the computer.

Despite these admonitions, it seems quite safe to predict that the computer will continue to expand social scientists' capacity to process vast quantities of information with speed and precision, and for that reason alone will persist in having an impact on contemporary research. Consequently, either social scientists learn to handle the machine or they risk being left behind by the discipline.

VOCATIONAL OPPORTUNITIES

An understanding of quantitative research, including computer procedures, prepares a person for a variety of positions in the labor market. Almost everyone is familiar with the fact that educational, business, and research institutions use computers extensively. Knowledge of computer-oriented research, hence, is an essential prerequisite for any person working for such private and public organizations. Investigators are employed in the areas of accounting, finance, management, marketing, and production. Such research activities, more often than not, utilize techniques which are dependent either wholly or partly on the computer. To be competitive, therefore, an individual must have some experience with quantitative research.

Often overlooked are the number of jobs available in federal, state, and local government. Many of these positions require persons who have at least an elementary comprehension of computer operations, even though some officials, especially at the local level, tend to be reluctant to apply quantitative analysis to their workaday operations. Since data are readily accessible from a variety of sources such as census information, governmental statistics, and official reports of quasigovernmental and private agencies, even the most hesitant officials are beginning to employ quantitative analysts in departments of public works, and in welfare, education, public-health, and motor-vehicle agencies, to name a few. Such agencies are potentially fertile areas of employment for persons who can couple computer operations with substantive knowledge. Understanding the logic of research, uses of the computer, and methods of report writing are becoming essential requirements for governmental employment.

Even though some governmental officials frequently are reluctant to adopt quantitative analytical techniques, many administrative authorities suggest that current trends will cause these officials to rely increasingly on computer-oriented analysis. Edward Hearle and Raymond Mason contend that there are eight recognizable and irrevocable trends occurring at the federal, state, and local levels of government which will force officials to use quantitative analysis. These trends are as follows:

1. Population will increase, particularly in urban areas.
2. State and local government services will expand, probably faster than population growth.
3. Within the organization of state and local government agencies, the leadership and control of the central

executive officer will increase, and consequently the independence of functional departments will decrease.

4. There will be continued expansion in intergovernmental relationships.

5. Some form of area government for dealing with metropolitan problems will evolve in many places.

6. Certain functions will expand rapidly as state and local governments respond to demands for public services.

7. Revenues to support these growing services will continue to be scarce, and it seems likely that the broader revenue base available to state governments will be drawn upon increasingly to provide support by means of subventions to local governments for functions performed at the local level.

8. The administration of state and local governments will become more professional.[3]

These forecasts suggest that governmental institutions, which admittedly change slowly, will require professional personnel who can work with quantitative data. For governmental agencies, like other organizations, the computer is as much a necessity as the automobile because the interaction between the current state of technology and public expectations compels decision makers to utilize the most efficient equipment available in order to process public demands quickly.[4]

Since any attempt to recite all the ways in which a computer is used in the public sector would be not only imprac-

[3]Edward Hearle and Raymond Mason, *A Data Processing System for State and Local Governments* (Englewood Cliffs, N.J.: Prentice-Hall, 1963), pp. 25–27. Reprinted by permission of publisher and the Rand Corporation.

[4]For a more developed view, see Harry H. Fite, *The Computer Challenge to Urban Planners and State Administrators* (Washington: Spartan Books, 1965).

tical but also futile, the following list merely presents some of the areas in which computer operations are used more frequently.

1. *General public administration and public management:* to keep track of budgets, appropriations, revenues, payrolls, property assessments, taxes, customer billing, bid letting and bid checking, report preparation
2. *City planning:* to process data concerning housing, population distribution, renewal contracts, land use, transportation facilities, travel demand
3. *Judicial administration:* to inventory moving and parking violations, criminal records, licensing records
4. *Public health, welfare, and safety:* to design, compute, and analyze delivery systems, medical payment procedures, engineering problems
5. *Traffic and transportation:* to ratiocinate maintenance scheduling, vehicle licensing, studies and surveys of traffic flows

The principal conclusion to be drawn from this abbreviated inventory is that computers are used for a wide range of governmental functions. Thus, the employee who enters the labor market without at least a fledgling knowledge of the computer and quantitative research is at a distinct disadvantage.

PURPOSE OF THE BOOK

The aim of this volume is to acquaint individuals with general guidelines needed to understand an electronic computing system, to operate statistical packages, and to write a respectable research report. The need for such a text is obvious when one stops to appraise the rapidly increasing emphasis being placed on the utilization of quantitative research in the social sciences. This relatively nontechnical book, therefore, is devised both as a supplementary text for novice researchers and as a guide for nonresearchers who wish to evaluate quantitative investigations, even though their knowledge of such endeavors is quite limited. Toward this end, the book concentrates on three integral elements of quantitative research. First, persons are introduced to the basic components of a computer. Only when individuals understand the logic of how a computer works can they use the machine efficiently. Second, prospective researchers are acquainted with various programmed statistical packages. Inasmuch as novice investigators usually do not possess the skills needed to write complicated computer instructions, the book introduces researchers to the least amount of information necessary to use (and analyze the results from) machines which process and calculate data efficiently, so that meaningful research may be conducted with a minimum of technical knowledge. Finally, beginners are exposed to some elementary rules that must be followed when communicating a project's findings via the written word. Although there admittedly is no step-by-step approach to writing quantitative reports, the reader is introduced to a simple sequential framework which hopefully will aid novices in writing their first report. By introducing the neophyte to computer equipment, package programs, and research-report writing, this book seeks to overcome computer and research illiteracy found among fledgling social scientists.

While there is a plethora of books pertaining to research methods, most of them, unfortunately, fail to explain exactly how the computer is utilized in the research process. More to the point, there is a dearth of short, simple texts showing beginners how to conduct and write research reports which rely on the computer. For the most part, available volumes, though admittedly they are fairly understandable to experienced social scientists, are altogether too complex and hence incomprehensible for the novice. A book that covers in detail every possible major research facet tends to defeat its purpose because beginners cannot comprehend much of what is discussed. They need a simplified text with which to start understanding the research process.

A simplified book, though indispensable, nevertheless presents problems. On one hand, such a work normally is subject to severe criticism by experts who see a danger in oversimplification. On the other hand, it is likely to be accepted uncritically by novices who are seeking pat answers. Neither view is realistic. Experts quickly forget the difficulty they had conducting and writing up their first quantitative research. Such experts often expect the research initiate to become a journeyman after reading a single complex methodology book. On the other side of the fence, the novice wants a text that spoon-feeds him to the point where a report can be written by merely filling in some blanks. He does not want to struggle to learn to use the computer creatively in quantitative research. This book addresses itself to the serious research tenderfoot who wants to learn, but has absolutely no knowledge about the computer. After reading and understanding the volume, he will be ready to tackle some complex methodology books. The reader also will be less likely to misuse quantitative and statistical techniques or reach faulty conclusions if he understands the basics presented between these covers.

At this point, a word of caution is appropriate. The text assumes that the reader has no prior exposure to the subject of computers or report writing. Thus, to keep the work simple, many important components of research have been omitted. The most critical intentional oversight is a discussion of theory as it is related to quantitative research. While the computer has given the social scientist the ability to manipulate large quantities of data, it in no way has diminished the need for research based on logically developed and defensible theories. After all, most research errors are the results of improper theoretical formulations, not incorrect calculations. Stated another way, illogical outcomes are the product of inaccurate theory, not the computer. Consequently, the user of this volume should frequently consult standard methodology books.

Given the complexity and diversity of research, it is impossible to develop such a process fully in an introductory volume. But a useful start can be made toward understanding the way in which a computer can contribute to quantitative research. While research seldom, if ever, is conducted sequentially, the step-by-step approach used in this book helps capture the flow of the research process. Since the book is designed as a supplementary text, additional steps can be introduced when needed. The subsequent discussion, therefore, is intended to provide the reader with an understanding of the computer and its application to the writing of research reports. As with all introductory books, its value depends to a large extent on the motivation, creativity, and imagination of the user.

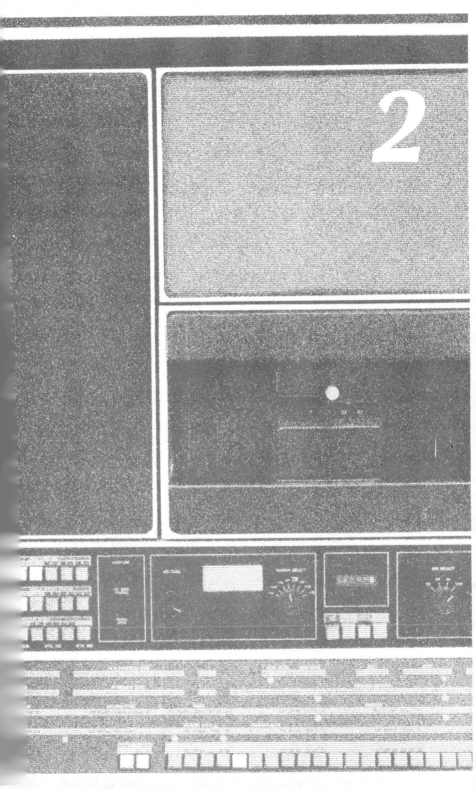

Understanding the Computer and Its Components

When a considerable number of cases are being examined, the investigator must store the information in a form in which it can be analyzed substantively and repeatedly for the purpose of eventually writing a meaningful report. Data usually are saved in the computer so they can be retrieved and manipulated easily whenever the researcher wishes. To be able to use this highly complex and flexible electronic device, one need not know all the intricacies of sophisticated computer programming techniques. It is sufficient to be able to manipulate the machine with programs that already are written.[1] (These prewritten programs will be

[1]Peter B. Harkins et al., *Introduction to Computer Programming for the Social Sciences* (Boston: Allyn and Bacon, 1973), p. 5. Reprinted by permission of publisher.

17

discussed in some detail in the next chapter.) Investigators, however, cannot learn to instruct computers with prewritten programs unless they understand at least the rudimentary workings of the machine; thus such a comprehension is an essential prerequisite for conducting quantitative research. Keeping this in mind, the objective of this chapter is to acquaint persons with basic concepts and components of computers and computing by discussing key features of the computer.

Before such features can be presented, however, a few cursory remarks about computers are necessary. A computer, it should be remembered, is a machine, usually electronic, which is directed by a programmed set of instructions to calculate arithmetical and logical functions sequentially. Within this definition, there are basically two general types of computers. One is a *special-purpose computer*, which is designed to perform limited functions for a single application (e.g., addressing envelopes). This machine is wired to execute identical operations every time; hence it is nonprogrammable. The only way such a computer can accomplish a task other than that for which it was constructed is to change the wiring system of the machine. The other type of computer is a *general-purpose computer*, a machine which can perform a wide variety of functions merely by programming it with different sets of instructions. Such a computer is extremely flexible and therefore is the most popular type of computer used in social research. Consequently, this chapter discusses only mechanisms associated with general-purpose (programmed) computers. (For a definition of computer and computing terms, see the Glossary.)

Although there are two families of general-purpose electronic computers—*analog* and *digital*—only the latter, which uses numbers or digits to perform computing functions, is treated in this volume. (Briefly, analog computers solve problems by translating numbers into physical conditions such as length and voltage, manipulating these physical conditions, and finally retranslating those conditions into numerical equivalents. Persons interested in analog computers should consult any of the various comprehensive computer textbooks.) Digital computers generally store information and execute calculations with one of the simplest communication schemes conceivable, commonly referred to as a *binary system*. In such a system, only two digits, 0 and 1, are used. Combinations of these digits represent all possible letters, numbers, and symbols. Several binary systems are in use; Table 2.1 demonstrates how one such basic numbering system works.

The computer does not actually store, either temporarily or permanently, the 0's and 1's. Instead, when a 1 is fed into the machine, the digit is converted into a positive electronic

TABLE 2.1 Common binary system

Decimal	Binary
0	0
1	1
2	10
3	11
4	100
5	101
6	110
7	111
8	1000
9	1001
10	1010
•	•
•	•
•	•
50	110010
•	•
•	•
•	•
150	10010110

current. When a 0 is entered, a negative electronic impulse is generated. Thus, a series of currents is entered, stored, and retrieved in the computer rather than digits, characters, or symbols.

Equipped with this information about different types of computers and the way data and instructions are entered into the machine, even the reader who has virtually no knowledge of digital electronic computers now is ready for a cursory presentation of a computer system, the major components of which are *input devices, storage units,* a *central processing unit,* and *output devices* (see Figure 2.1).

INPUT DEVICES

Before data are stored in the computer for immediate and future use, they must be transformed into electrical impulses by an input mechanism. At present, the most commonly used input device employed by the social researcher is the *punched card,* a three by eight inch card perforated by a punching machine (see Figure 2.2). The presence or ab-

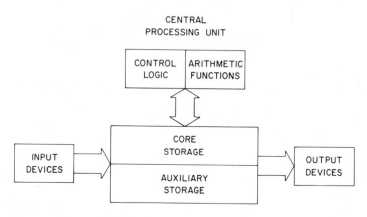

Figure 2.1 **Basic components of a computer.**

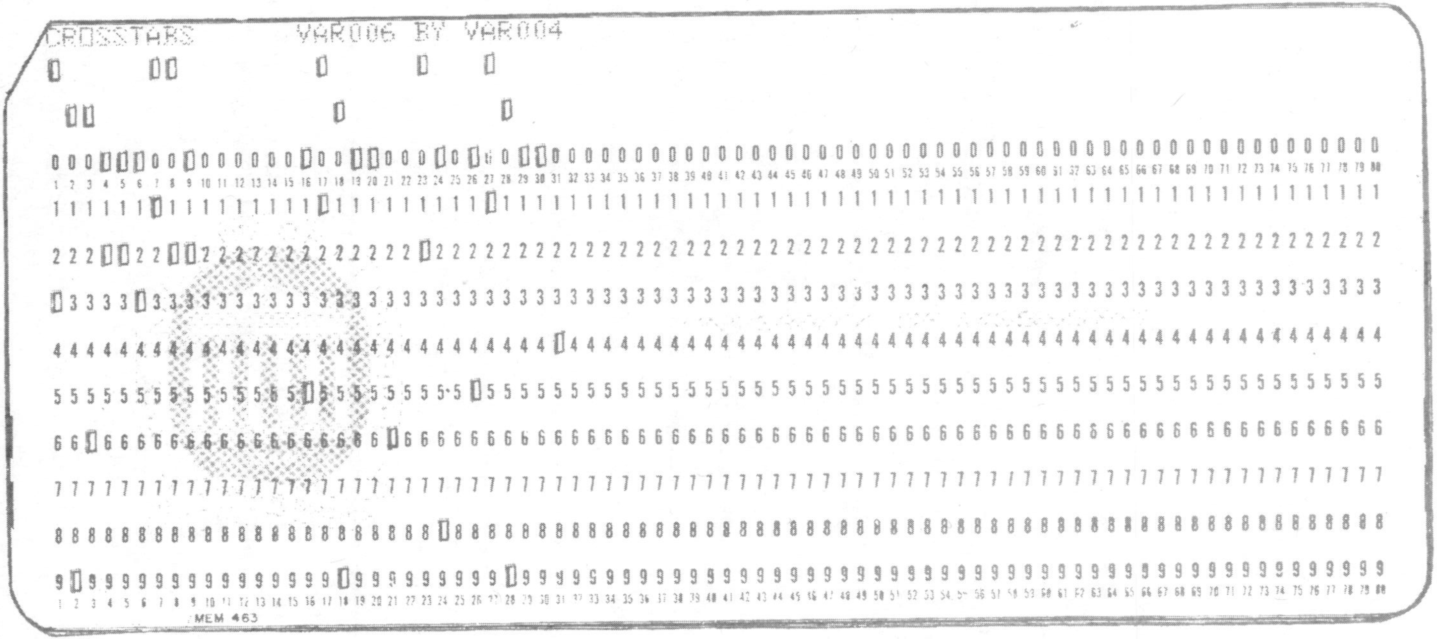

Figure 2.2 A punched card. [COURTESY OF INTERNATIONAL BUSINESS MACHINES CORPORATION]

sence of holes in particular columns of the card is interpreted by the computer as a specific and useful particle of information.

Today the two most extensively used devices for punching holes in computer cards are *keypunching* and *mark-sensing* machines. Mark sensing, which is a considerably faster technique than keypunching, involves marking specific predetermined positions on the card with an ordinary lead pencil. Holes then are punched in these marked cards via a fiber-optics process. Simply put, a light is transmitted from a source through glass fibers to a scanning station. As each card passes over the light beam, a punching machine is activated by the marks and holes are punched in the appropriate places in the card. The most frequently used method by which holes are punched in cards, however, is not mark sensing but keypunching, a process which is accomplished by a punching machine that looks like a carriageless typewriter (see Figure 2.3). (For an example of keypunching techniques, see Appendix A.) Holes are punched manually in the proper column as the card passes through the punching station.

After the cards are punched, they are read into the computer by means of a *card reader* (Figure 2.4), a machine which scans cards as rapidly as 1000 per minute. The reader senses the punched holes as the card passes between a light source and photoelectric cells. Data, read one column at a time, are transformed into electronic impulses and transmitted to buffer storage until the reading process is completed, whereupon they are transferred to the computer's core or auxiliary storage units.

Another input mechanism commonly employed by the social scientist to enter data and instructions into the computer is the *teletype* (Figure 2.5), a device that resembles an electric typewriter. The user types information into the computer by means of a keyboard on the teletype. At that time, the

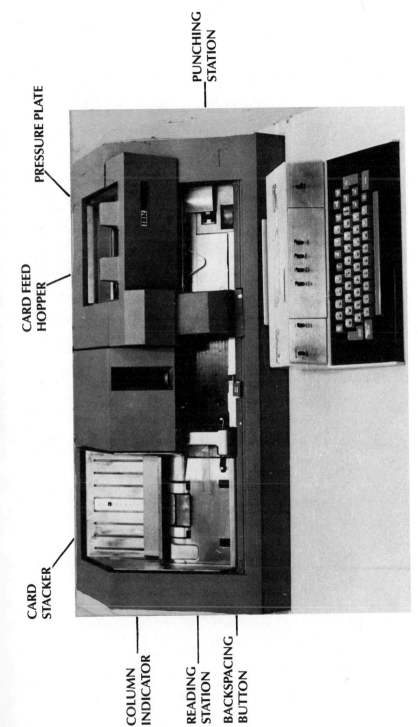

Figure 2.3 Keypunch. [Courtesy of International Business Machines Corporation]

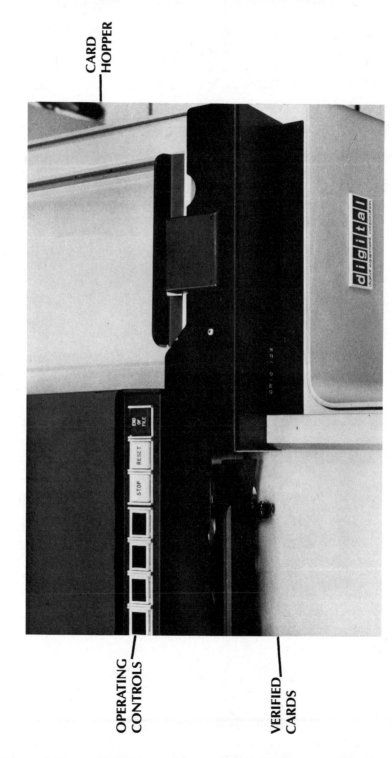

Figure 2.4 Card reader.

CHARACTER DISPLAY

KEYBOARD

Figure 2.5 Teletype terminal

information in the form of electronic impulses is transmitted and compiled in the computer storage units.

When users submit data and instructions to the computer by means of card input, they generally are using a procedure called *batch processing*. Utilizing batch mode, a person punches all instructions onto computer cards, then feeds that information through a card reader to the computer, which compiles the statements and executes them sequentially without further aid from the user. In contrast, there is another input mode, called *time sharing*, which allows the user to interact with programmed instructions at any stage of their execution. In other words, the user can interrupt and change sequential instructions any time he desires. Such an option is not available when employing batch processing.

Of the two modes of input, beginners probably will use batch processing, for two reasons. In the first place, the novice is likely to use prewritten programs (such as those discussed in Chapter 3), and such programs operate only via batch mode. Secondly, batch processing is more efficient than time sharing. Since the user does not have to be present when commands are issued to the machine, batch-submitted programs can be run during the computer's slack hours when rates are lower (e.g., midnight). Because beginners tend to use batch input instead of time sharing, the discussion and examples of program instructions cited in this book will pertain to batch processing.

STORAGE DEVICES

All digital computers are designed to operate with some kind of storage device, which is a mechanism where information is kept so it can be retrieved when needed. Such information always is saved in the form of a file, a collection of related data and instructions located in a particular area on a storage device. Not all computers, it should be noted, have identical storage capacity. The size and capacity of the storage device normally determine the amount of information that can be banked within a system at any one time.[2] As F. R. Crawford states, "Storage capacity varies with the computer system to which the file is attached, since different machines use different coding schemes and record formats".[3]

Information is stored on one of two basic types of storage devices, *core* and *auxiliary*. The core storage mechanism is a magnetic hub, a small doughnut-shaped ferromagnetic element less than one-hundredth of an inch in size. In the core memory system, of which there are hundreds of thousands in large computers, the ferromagnetic planes (see Figure 2.6) are subjected to a magnetic field by means of an electric current. After the current saturates the metal, bits of binary information are stored on the device by magnetization. (Recall the discussion about how the computer converts binary numbers into electronic impulses.)

For the social scientist, who permanently saves considerable amounts of data, auxiliary storage units usually are needed. Researchers for the most part utilize either magnetic tape or magnetic disk as an auxiliary storage mechanism, inasmuch as both have approximately the same capacity for holding data.[4] Data normally are punched onto cards which are read into the computer and saved on either tape or disk.

---

[2] The size of a computer's memory system usually is measured in K bytes, which are units of 1024 bytes. Thus a computer with a capacity core of 128 K has 131,072 bytes of memory.

[3] F. R. Crawford, *Introduction to Data Processing* (Englewood Cliffs, N.J.: Prentice-Hall, 1968), p. 199. Reprinted by permission of publisher.

[4] Although tapes and disks are considered input and output devices, they are used essentially for storing large amounts of data because the computer's core memory has limited capacity to retain information.

CORES

Figure 2.6 Core planes.

From then on, data are accessed directly from the auxiliary storage mechanism.

Tape

Of the two types of auxiliary devices, the magnetic tape is used most frequently to store large quantities of demountable reference data.[5] Information is stored on tape when a reel, a plastic spool resembling those used to hold movie film, is mounted on a tape drive (Figure 2.7) and the tape runs across magnetic reading and writing heads, much like a film in a movie projector. The writing heads consist of magnetic elements placed perpendicular to the tape. The tape contains magnetic particles in the oxide coating capable of retaining magnetism until remagnetized. As the tape passes by the writing heads, the information in the form of positive and negative impulses remagnetizes the tape, thus storing the data.

Tapes are extremely popular storage devices because they can hold so much information. In fact, more than one file can be stored on a single tape. When this occurs, a special character called a tape mark is placed at the end of each file by the computer. This mark signals the tape drive to prepare for the end of one file and the beginning of another.

The following list of operations is designed to help the beginner understand the process by which a computer writes on and reads from a magnetic tape.

WRITING
1. A fraction of a second is required to accelerate the tape to the proper speed.

---

[5]Magnetic tapes come in two sizes: 1200 or 2400 feet long and ½ inch wide. More often than not, the computer uses nine-track oxide-coated tape which records information at 800 bytes per inch (b.p.i.). To the layman, this means that 100 unblocked cards will occupy nearly 85 inches of tape. Viewed another way, a 2400-foot tape written at a density of 800 b.p.i. can hold 20 million characters of information.

MACHINE REEL

FILE REEL

READ-WRITE HEADS

Figure 2.7   Tape mounted on tape drive.

2. Data are transmitted to the writing heads, column by column, from core storage while the tape is moving.
3. The data are recorded magnetically on the tape.
4. When all the data in the file have been recorded, the computer sends a special signal to the drive, which produces an end-of-file mark on the tape.
5. At the end of data transmission, the tape is stopped by the computer. But, since motion cannot start or stop instantaneously, the tape decelerates for another very small fraction of a second.
6. When an end-of-reel mark is encountered, the computer is notified to rewind the tape.

READING

1. The computer starts the tape drive in motion when it is ready to receive data.
2. The drive takes a fraction of a second to reach proper operating speed. Data sensed by the read heads are transmitted, column by column, to core storage.
3. The drive continues to send data to the computer until it reaches the end-of-file mark which indicates the transmission completion. Taking a fraction of a second to stop tape motion, the drive stops.
4. If the file has more than one reel, an end-of-file signal tells the computer to rewind the tape. Either the operator loads the next reel or the computer may switch to an alternate unit where the next reel is ready.[6]

Disk

Another auxiliary storage device social scientists utilize is the disk, a thin magnetically coated platter closely resembling a phonograph record. The disk, which provides

[6]Crawford, pp. 183–184.

greater flexibility for handling stored data than does tape, is mounted on a vertical shaft like a phonograph record (Figure 2.8). As the disk rotates on a turntable, two read-write heads situated on a movable arm enable information to be read from or written onto a revolving disk.[7] Binary data are stored on a disk in a manner similar to that which is used with tape.

Disks are regarded as direct-access devices because the read-write heads can be placed anywhere on the disk. For instance, assume for a moment that the requested file X is located between two other files on the same auxiliary mechanism. In order for the computer to retrieve and process file X from a tape, the first portion of the tape which contains the first file has to be scanned until the second and requested file is found. When file X is stored between two files on a disk, the read-write heads can move directly to a desired position and reference the requested file without scanning through the first file on the disk. In addition to the advantage of direct access, a file stored on a disk, unlike one stored on tape, does not have to be rewound after it is used, thus saving computer time and money.

Not only are magnetic tapes and disks light, compact, and durable, but they also are economical, since the devices can be erased automatically merely by writing new information over old. (This feature, however, requires extra care when storing data, since one can unintentionally destroy information by writing over it.) As a result of being able to reuse these mechanisms, the user is provided with auxiliary stor-

---

[7]Physically speaking, each disk has 200 tracks. A track is a concentric groove located on the disk's surface. Each track has room for slightly more than 7000 characters. Ordinarily, a single disk does not appear as part of a storage unit. Rather, ten disks are bound together to form a disk pack. Data then can be stored not only on tracks but also on units called cylinders, which consist of one track from both the bottom and top surface of each of the ten disks (i.e. 20 tracks).

READ-WRITE HEADS

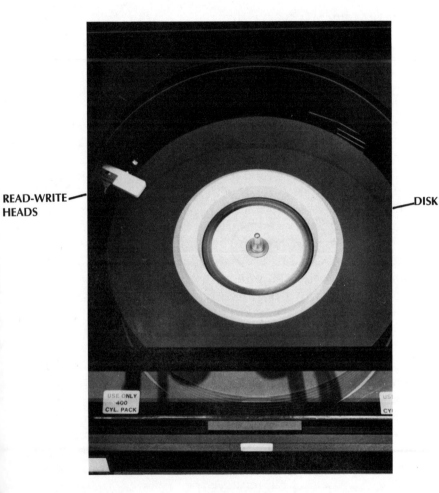

DISK

Figure 2.8   Mounted disk pack.

age of high capacity, swift access, and considerable flexibility, making tapes and disks almost perfect storage devices.

CENTRAL PROCESSING UNIT

Once data are stored, the computer has to be given a set of instructions which tells it how to manipulate them. Such functions are performed by the *central processing unit* (CPU), that part of the computer which contains mechanisms for locating, retrieving, and calculating data. (One such unit is shown in Figure 2.9.) Since the computer executes instructions in billionths of a second, calculations normally require less time than do input and output operations, because the latter functions require mechanical devices that work slower than the electronic mechanisms that compute and process information. Therefore, a considerable amount of time is wasted when the computer has to stand idle during input or output operations. Rather than waste valuable time, the CPU directs the computer to input many programs virtually concurrently. In the meantime, output solutions are read into buffer storage and held there until all mechanical operations are completed, thereby freeing electronic components to process other waiting jobs. Operating in this manner, the CPU allows the computer to function efficiently.

The CPU includes a *control unit*, an *arithmetic-logic unit*, and *registers*. The control unit is that part of the machine that stores and implements the user's instructions. The arithmetic-logic unit contains the electronic circuitry that permits the computer to perform actual computations such as adding, subtracting, multiplying, dividing, transferring, and comparing. The registers are temporary units utilized for saving various calculations which are needed for later computations.

Other than the aforementioned general components, the

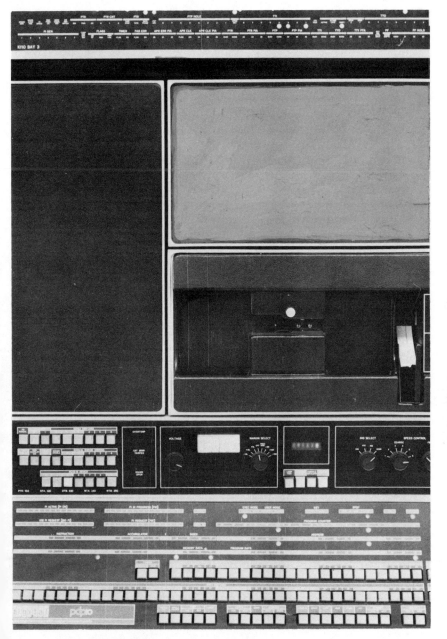

Figure 2.9   Central processing unit.

details of the CPU are too complicated to be of use to the neophyte using packaged statistical programs. It is sufficient to realize that this portion of the computer is by far the most complex, but need not be of primary concern to the user, since "canned" programs incorporate precise detailed instructions necessary to direct the CPU.

OUTPUT DEVICES

After data are processed, the requested information is transmitted to the user via one or more output devices. The two most popular output devices are *printers* and *punched cards*. Printers receive output from core storage in the form of electronic impulses which in turn activate printing elements, causing them to type characters (alphabetic, numeric, and special) on paper. Two types of printers dominate the current market, *character printers* and *line printers*. Character printers, which are relatively inexpensive, operate like a typewriter, printing the characters one at a time. Line printers (Figure 2.10), on the other hand, type all characters on a line almost simultaneously. All the characters are assembled in a type chain before a magnetic hammer that presses the paper against the chain. For comparison, line printers reach speeds up to 2000 lines per minute, whereas character printers go no faster than 600 lines per minute.

Another output device is the punched card, a medium which usually is used when small quantities of information are produced as input data for other programs. With the exception that there are no characters printed at the top of the card, an output card is exactly like an input card. Consequently, punched-card output has to be run through an interpreting machine if printing at the top of the card is needed.

Other more sophisticated but less frequently employed

PRINTING
MECHANISM

PAPER
FEED

Figure 2.10   Line printer.

output devices are available to the social scientist. Among them are a variety of plotters that produce solution data in graphic form. In particular, the cathode-ray tube (CRT), an apparatus which presents output visually on a screen similar to a small television set (Figure 2.11), is well suited for social research.

PROGRAMMING

As previously mentioned, data processing involves placing data in the computer, manipulating them to produce results, and transmitting the output to the user for judgment. To perform such actions, the computer must be given a set of instructions, conventionally called a program, which generally directs the machine to move data from storage to the computing unit where arithmetic-logic functions are conducted and back to storage where output is produced for user analysis. Figure 2.12 schematically shows the flow of a data-processing cycle.

To accomplish programming tasks, the computer must be told exactly what to do in a way that it can understand. As the English language permits persons to communicate with each other, programming languages permit the user to issue commands to the computer. Such pasigraphies direct the machine to perform specific iterative functions. However, not all instructions are processed in their order of appearance. Under particular conditions sequencing commands often direct the machine to choose from a series of alternative sets of instructions. This capability is the heart of the computer's ability to solve problems.

Generally speaking, the computer is given instructions in one of two families of programming languages, *symbolic* and *problem-solving*. Whereas symbolic languages are nonnumerical expressions, problem-solving languages are algebraically written terms. Of the two, problem-solving

CHARACTER DISPLAY

ENTRY KEYBOARD

Figure 2.11 Cathode-ray-tube terminal.

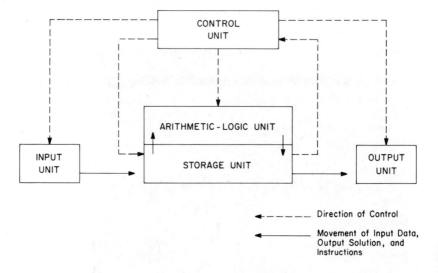

Figure 2.12 Data-processing cycle. [Source: Paul Emrick and Joseph Wilkinson, *Computer Programming for Business and Social Science* (Homewood, Illinois: Dorsey Press, 1970), p. 10.]

languages are used most frequently because they reduce the time and effort involved in program writing and require fewer commands than do symbolic languages. The two most utilized problem solving languages are FORTRAN (FORmula TRANslation) and COBOL (COmmon Business Oriented Language).[8] Regardless of which of the two languages is used, orders are given to the computer in the form of *input instructions, compute directions,* and *output commands.* Input instructions direct the processing unit to read data from an external storage medium such as cards, tape, or disk and place those data in core storage. The compute di-

---

[8]Inasmuch as problem-solving languages contain written statements similar to English, they have to be translated into digital language by a program referred to as a compiler before the computer can understand user instructions.

rections pilot the computer's processing plant in performing specified arithmetic-logic operations and store the results in an assigned space within core storage. Finally, output commands tell the machine to retrieve the calculated values from storage and produce them on an output device.

In the past, programming the computer was a time-consuming and vastly complex affair. However, with the development of readily available and inexpensive prewritten statistical packages, the social scientist is able to manipulate the machine with a minimum of programming knowledge. These prewritten programs make it unnecessary to write complex programs whenever the user wishes to solve problems or manipulate data. Moreover, prewritten procedures free the user for less repetitious and more challenging tasks.

CONCLUDING COMMENT

As this brief introduction to computer features shows, the machine is a potentially powerful tool which can effectively facilitate the research process only when the user has a clear conception of how the computer works. It should be understood that the computer is limited to the extent that it depends on human direction. Yet, when properly used, the machine frees skillful investigators from time consuming computational tasks, thereby increasing the potential for creative analysis.

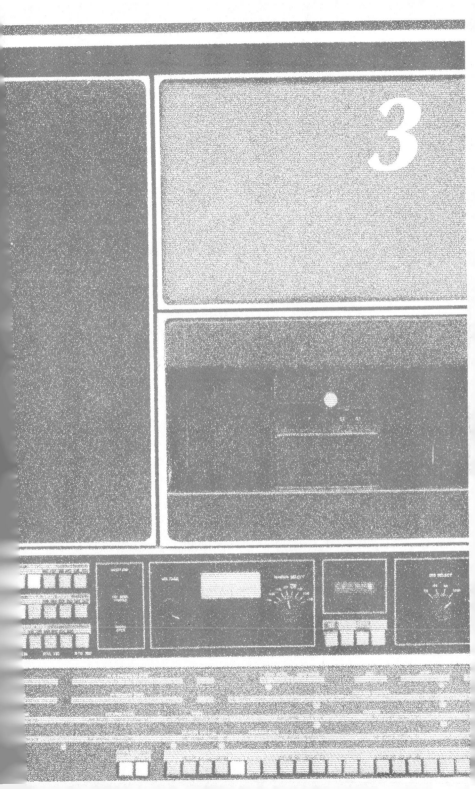

Programming
with a Statistical Package

Despite the computer's complexity, most investigators need not know a great deal about programming to be able to handle the machine, because over the past few years prewritten packaged statistical programs which make it possible to direct the electronic digital computer with a minimum of programming skill have been developed. Such packages consist of a combination of frequently used manipulative and statistical procedures which are written and stored in the computer for future use. Consequently, it is unnecessary to write a detailed set of instructions every time one wants to tell the computer to execute particular functions. The user merely has to access the stored operating instructions, and they will direct the machine to perform the desired manipulations. Since such accessing directives (being designed for beginners) usually are quite simple and straightforward, a person needs to know only a few relatively elementary programming routines to activate any procedure in a statistical package.

Though a wide variety of packages are available, all prewritten programs have certain characteristics in common. In the first place, they have almost identical sets of prewritten procedures. For instance, all packages enable users to issue commands to transform data, manipulate files, and calculate various types of statistics. These prewritten operations allow beginners to modify files (either permanently or temporarily), generate new variables, and compute various descriptive statistics such as frequency distributions, cross-tabulation matrices, and simple correlation coefficients. For experienced analysts, the packages contain sophisticated techniques such as partial correlation analysis, analysis of variance, multiple regression analysis, discriminant analysis, factor analysis, and canonical analysis, to name a few.

Another property packaged programs have in common is a set of integrated control statements which permit a person to access a variety of procedures with basically the same format. Such statements are a group of commands which direct the computer to retrieve and use stored programs in a manner the user desires. Inasmuch as the control-statement format is virtually identical for all programs in a particular package, each program can be written with a minimum of programming knowledge. In other words, once a package's basic format is understood, any of the programs can be accessed with only a few changes in the control statements.

Although the format of control statements varies among packages, the basic types of directives found in all programs are as follows:

1. *Keyword commands* activate specific programs in the package. In SPSS, to cite an example, the keyword FRE-

46

QUENCIES directs the computer to calculate frequency distributions.

2. *Specification commands* set parameters on keyword commands. For instance, when a cross-tabulation table is requested, the specification statement itemizes the variables to be cross-tabulated.

3. *Delimiter commands* separate keywords and specification statements and items within specification statements. The three most frequently utilized delimiters are the blank, comma, and slash.

4. *Option commands* allow certain standard manipulative and statistical procedures to be chosen from the package's repertoire. Statements selecting statistical procedures are illustrations of option commands.

Still another feature of programmed packages is their natural-language format, a characteristic which is particularly beneficial to persons without programming skill. A natural-language format means that programming statements are written in unmistakable everyday English. In contrast, nonpackage programs generally are written in a problem-solving language such as FORTRAN or COBOL. Using such language means that instructions are issued in a detailed and sequential mathematical format. By way of illustration, an SPSS natural-language keyword command directing the computer to calculate a Pearson's product moment correlation is simply PEARSON CORR. On the other hand, a problem-solving command telling the machine to compute a Yule's Q looks in part like this:

$$Q = (A * D - B * C)/(A * D + B * C).$$

Of course, beginners must keep in mind that natural-language statements actually instruct the computer to retrieve and use stored procedures which are written in problem-solving language. Thus, in the end, problem-solving language always is used to execute desired funtions. Rather than write such commands, however, the user just has to access them with a package's appropriate natural-language statements.

The easy accessibility and manageability of packaged programs has led to two prevalent abuses, overuse and misapplication. There is a tendency for novices (and others for that matter) to "go on fishing expeditions," that is, to request the computer to calculate a large number of different statistical functions in the hope of inducing worthwhile output. The rule of thumb for any beginner is to access only those functions that are needed to test a hypothesis, a speculated relationship based on theoretical formulations. The second misemployment of packaged programs occurs when statistics with which users are unfamiliar are requested. A person often desires to use the most powerful statistical tool available, even when data do not meet the requirements for the statistics. Generally speaking, inexperienced investigators should not use statistics they do not understand or cannot interpret. Citing these two abuses, however, is not meant to deter exploratory research. This discussion merely is intended to suggest that to prevent a waste of time and effort one needs to determine his research strategy before using prewritten packaged programs.

OVERVIEW OF SELECTED PACKAGES

The three most comprehensive, flexible, and popular prewritten manipulative and statistical packages used by social scientists are *Statistical Package for the Social Sciences* (SPSS), *Organized Set of Integrated Routines for Investigation with Statistics* (OSIRIS), and *Biomedical Computer Programs* (BMD).[1] SPSS, which became available to the public in the late 1960s after being developed earlier by a group of social scientists, computer scientists, and statisticians working at Stanford University, is an intergrated system of combined statistical procedures designed to preform various types of quantitative analyses. (Since the early 1970s, however, the SPSS project has been housed in the National Opinion Research Center at the University of Chicago.) The main objective of SPSS is to provide a set of manipulative and statistical operations that can be handled easily by computer-naive social scientists. The package furnishes the neophyte with an almost unlimited capability for manipulating, transforming, and modifying existing data. This comprehensive set of programmed procedures includes the following functions:

1. Various descriptive statistics
2. Frequency distributions
3. Cross-tabulation matrices
4. Simple and multiple correlations
5. Scatter diagrams
6. Partial correlations
7. Means and variances for stratified populations
8. Analyses of variance and covariance
9. Simple and multiple regression analysis
10. Discriminant analysis
11. Factor analysis
12. Canonical analysis
13. Guttman scaling

Besides performing these tasks, SPSS has the ability to generate new variables from a combination of older ones; to delete, combine, recode, and collapse existent varables; to

[1]The following descriptions of the prewritten packages are extrapolated from their respective manuals: Norman Nie et al., *Statistical Package for the Social Sciences* (New York: McGraw-Hill, 1975); Institute for Social Research, OSIRIS III (Ann Arbor: University of Michigan, 1973); and W. J. Dixon (ed.), *Biomedical Computer Programs* (Berkeley: University of California Press, 1975).

categorize, select, or weigh specific cases; and to add variables to a file. The SPSS manual, a thoroughly comprehensible and readable book, explains in more detail the techniques available in the package.

OSIRIS, developed originally in the late 1950s by the Institute for Social Research (ISR) at the University of Michigan, is used primarily for statistical tabulation and multivariate analyses. Since the package evolved from survey research projects conducted by ISR, the primary objective of OSIRIS always has been to provide users with a combination of procedures for editing data and applying multivariate analyses to the Institute's aggregate data collections. Once the Institute began documenting data and disseminating them to various computer installations, particularly to computer centers at other universities, the developers of OSIRIS by necessity expanded the number of prewritten programs in the package's repertoire.

The OSIRIS software package, which like all packages has been expanding over the years, now has an extensive array of capabilities. Its major functions include the ability to:

1. Organize and edit card image data
2. Copy and subset data
3. Transform data values
4. Generate univariate and bivariate frequency distributions and related statistics
5. Produce scatter plots
6. Perform correlational analysis
7. Perform multiple regression analysis
8. Perform multivariate analysis of variance
9. Conduct multivariate analysis with nominal, ordinal, or metric variables
10. Factor analyze data
11. Conduct multidimensional scaling
12. Perform cluster analysis

As in SPSS, each program can be executed separately or in a chain; that is, the output from one function can be fed as input to another. The OSIRIS manual discusses the implementation format for each program in the package.

BMD, designed by the UCLA Medical Center in the early 1960s for medical research, is used by social scientists because the multifarious statistical and mathematical procedures are conveniently adaptable to various types of social research. According to its developers, BMD programs, like SPSS and OSIRIS ones, are intended to permit researchers with a variety of data processing and statistical tasks to conduct desired computations with simple coded instructions. The stock BMD programs are:

1. Description and tabulations, producing various descriptive and bivariate correlations
2. Regression analysis, providing simple and multiple regression coefficients
3. Time-series analysis, generating statistics to examine change over time
4. Variance analysis, yielding coefficients for analyses of variance and covariance
5. Multivariate analysis, treating mathematical models such as factor analysis, discriminant analysis, and canonical analysis
6. Special programs, providing for Guttman scaling and techniques for transforming data.

Like SPSS and OSIRIS, these integrated BMD programs may be run in succession, with each program based on output from preceding analyses. All the necessary information is described in the manual, which should be consulted frequently when the package is used.

By now, it should be evident that all of these packages have identical objectives and perform basically the same manipulative and statistical functions. (In fact, the programs also have similar limitations, the major one being that the programmed procedures can only be activated via batch mode. As a result, interaction with a program while it is being executed is impossible. However, interactive packaged programs, though presently unavailable, are being developed.) There are, however, a few dissimilarities worth mentioning. Although some differences are too technical and intricate for beginners to grasp, others are fundamental and should be noted. In the first place, novices probably will find SPSS the easiest package to understand. Not only is the SPSS manual the most readable, but it also explains all the statistical operations available to the user, a feature not incorporated in either the OSIRIS or the BMD manual. Secondly, even though the packages contain approximately equivalent programs, each includes some unique functions. To take one instance, only OSIRIS can perform certain types of cluster analyses and multidimensional scaling and utilize multiple response variables. SPSS and BMD do not have such capabilities. Finally, when contrasting comparable versions of each package, OSIRIS and BMD can be used with smaller computing systems, accompanied, perhaps, by faster turnaround time.

After considering carefully major differences among the packages, it is difficult, if not impossible, to say which is best for beginners. The answer is contingent on the background and needs of each investigator. No single package, to be sure, can satisfy the requirements of all quantitative analysts, because each sequence of instructions has advantages and disadvantages, depending upon the user's level of methodological sophistication and statistical comprehension.

USING A STATISTICAL PACKAGE

When reading about computer components and operations, it often is easy to overlook the fact that the objective of such knowledge is to help one understand the machine and its symbiotic language enough to direct the computer to perform desired functions. (Otherwise, why read such a conglomeration of comparatively uninteresting material?) To demonstrate exactly how packaged programs are used to direct the computer to execute desired tasks, the remainder of this chapter discusses and illustrates some uses of the SPSS programmed package. SPSS was chosen for such a demonstration because the procedures, it is believed, are the easiest for computer novices to grasp. Armed with a few simple SPSS statements, beginners can tell the machine via batch mode to execute various manipulative and statistical functions.

To utilize SPSS (or for that matter any other package) for quantitative research, the novice has to know at least how to manipulate a stored data file by selecting only variables essential to the study and by recoding those variables into a usable form. Furthermore, he has to be able to order the computer to take selected variables and cross-tabulate them to produce a percentage table together with appropriate statistics, since both of these kinds of output are used extensively in quantitative analysis. Therefore, programs which enable a user to perform such operations will serve as illustrations of the way in which packaged procedures can be used.

When using SPSS, the programmer generally writes two sets of commands, job-control-language (JCL) statements and SPSS statements. JCL statements are a series of instructions that tell the computer what to do with the SPSS statements. The format, vocabulary, and syntax rules of JCL statements depend primarily upon the brand of computer used. Since it is impossible to cite examples for every brand of computer on the market today, JCL statements for computers made by International Business Machines (IBM) and Digital Electronic Corporation (DEC) have been selected as examples. These sample setups provide the reader with the basic knowledge needed to understand JCL statements, regardless of the type of computer the investigator employs. The second group of commands are SPSS statements, which retrieve prewritten programs that instruct the machine actually to execute certain manipulations and computations on selected variables in a stored file.

Job-Control-Language (JCL) Statements

Before a social scientist can adequately program a computer, he must know some elementary JCL statements. When using the computer, he might utilize the following JCL (and SPSS) statements.

```
DEC format.
$JOB FACTUR ¢1212,12! /TIME:00:10:00 /UNIQUE:1
$PASSWORD PLUM
$DECK JEH.SPS
RUN NAME    VGNDA
GET FILE    NAT.SPS.
PROCEDURE CARDS
FINISH
$EOD
$TOPS10
.RUN SPSS¢5,5!
DSK.LF=JEH.SPS
.Q DSK.LF /DI:D
$EOJ
```

In order of occurrence, each statement has the following meaning (explanations of SPSS system commands are marked with an asterisk [*]):

$JOB   notifies the computer to create a control file in which the succeeding commands are placed.

	The dollar sign tells the computer to execute the commands.
FACTUR	is any name the user desires to call the job that he has just initiated.
¢1212,12!	is the user's project number; the symbol ¢ is a left enclosed bracket ([), and the ! is a right enclosed bracket (]).
/	is a delimiter that ends one statement so that the user can begin another under the same command string.
TIME:00:10:00	is the estimated amount of CPU time the job will require, listed in hours, minutes, and seconds. The example indicates 10 minutes.
UNIQUE:1	is the number of batch jobs that can be run under the current project number: if 1, run only one batch job at a time; if 0, run any number of jobs under this project number.
$PASSWORD PLUM	are characters associated with the programmer's project number. If the punched password does not match the one stored under the programmer's project number, the job will not run. The example is PLUM.
$DECK JEH.SPS	specifies the particular name of a temporary input file consisting of SPSS commands. The name of the temporary file is JEH.SPS.

RUN NAME	VGNDA	*designates the name of the specific run: in this setup, VGNDA.
GET FILE	NAT.SPS	*tells the computer which file to access for the following set of manipulations. The name of the file must correspond to the file name of data already stored; in this case the file to be retrieved is NAT.SPS.
PROCEDURE CARDS		*vary with the type of SPSS program requested and will be discussed at greater length later in the chapter.
FINISH		*signifies the end of SPSS system commands.
$EOD		terminates the input that is being copied onto the temporary file. That is, it is the End Of the newly created Data file, JEH.SPS.
$TOPS10		creates temporary file for control file.
.RUN SPSS¢5,5!		commands the computer to run the SPSS package which is located on disk space 5,5. The period is the first character in a subcommand issued by the programmer.
DSK.LF=JEH.SPS		directs the computer to store output from the $DECK file in an output file named DSK.LF.
.Q DSK.LF		the Queue command, allows the programmer to use input or output devices—in this case, to take the output of the previously

manipulated data stored under the file name DSK.LF and print it on a line printer.

DI:D   tells the computer to DIspose and Delete the information stored for use by the line printer; in this example, a file named DSK.LF.

$EOJ   stops the computer; End Of Job.

IBM format.

```
//1212,12,'HY',TIME = 10
//  EXEC PGM = SPSS
//GO.FT03F001 DD VOL = SER = 240136,DSN = FIVNA, UNIT =
DISK
//  DISP = (OLD,KEEP), DCB = (LRECL = 80, BLKSIZE =
1600,RECFM = FB)
//GO.SYSIN DD*
RUN NAME   VGNDA
GET FILE   FIVNA
PROCEDURE CARDS
FINISH
/*
```

Each statement has the following meaning (explanations of SPSS commands are again marked with an asterisk *):

//   tells the computer to execute the following commands. When more than one card is needed to issue a command, the second card begins with two slashes followed by at least one blank space.

1212,12   notifies the computer to create a control file under the user's project number, 1212,12.

'HY'	is the user's name or code, listed for identification purposes. The user's name is HY.
TIME=10	estimates the amount of CPU time the job will require; listed in minutes, in this case 10 minutes.
// EXEC PGM=SPSS	tells the control file the ProGraM to be EXECuted is SPSS.
//GO.FT03F001	directs the computer to GO and get the SPSS file which is stored under the name FT03F001.
DD	is a Data Definition statement which describes the data file being used to run the job.
VOL=SER=240136	is the VOLume and SERial number of the disk on which data reside. The example is 240136.
DSN=FIVNA	gives the Data Set Name which is the name of the data file to be used. The illustrated name is FIVNA.
UNIT=DISK	indicates the device on which data are stored. The device in the example is DISK.
DISP=(OLD,KEEP)	indicates to the computer the DISPosition of the data before they are used and what to do with the data after they are used. In the illustration the file to be used is OLD and the computer is instructed to KEEP it after the program is run.
DCB=(LRECL=80, BLKSIZE=1600, RECFM=FB)	The Data Control Block lets the

computer know how much core space has to be set aside for data that are to be used. These specifications depend upon data format. LRECL stands for the Logical RECord Length, which for card image data is 80. BLKSIZE means BLocK SIZE and is always listed in multiples of the LRECL, in this case 1600. RECFM is RECord ForMat and usually is stated as FB, Fixed Block.

//G0.SYSIN DD* — instructs the computer to GO and retrieve the data as defined by Data Definition statements, put them INto a control file, and let the SYStem execute the commands.

RUN NAME   VGNDA — *designates the name of the specific run; in this setup, VGNDA.

GET FILE   FIVNA — *tells the computer which file to access for the following set of manipulations. The name of the file must correspond to the file name of data already stored; in this case the file to be retrieved is FIVNA.

PROCEDURE CARDS — *vary with the type of SPSS program requested and will be discussed at greater length later in the chapter.

FINISH — *signifies the end of SPSS system commands.

/* — stops the computer; end of job.

SPSS Statements

Besides understanding JCL statements, the user has to grasp the elements of SPSS statements, commands which are similar to conversational English.[2] Each SPSS statement consists of two parts: control comments located in columns 1–15 and specification expressions situated in columns 16–80+ (see Figure 3.1).

The control field contains particular keyword commands that direct the computer to perform specific manipulative and statistical functions. The specification field, which may be continued on as many cards as necessary provided an expression is not split and the remaining portion of the continued command begins in column 16, is the second part of the command string. Each set of instructions within the specification field ends with either a simple delimiter (blank column or comma) or a special delimiter (parenthesis or slash).

The keywords in the control field are restricted by the type of program the user wishes to initiate. That is, these are preprogrammed words, each of which generates particular manipulative and statistical procedures. The content and length of the specification field are up to the researcher provided he follows the conventions and limitations to which each program is subject. He directs the computer to execute actual manipulations and calculations by selecting an individual program and punching the appropriate keyword for the chosen SPSS program in the control field. Then, certain prescribed statements are placed in the specification field, comments which tell the computer the exact functions to be performed on specific variables.

[2]Nie et al., Chapter 3.

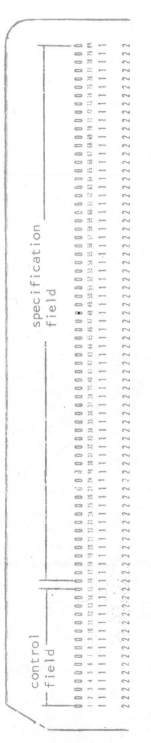

Figure 3.1 Format for an SPSS statement.

Specification keywords, like control keywords, are pre-determined characters that have special meaning in the SPSS system. Unlike control keywords, which activate only general operations, specification commands catalyze particular manipulative and statistical functions of the referenced SPSS program. For instance, the control keyword STATISTICS instructs the computer to calculate statistical functions, while the integers 1 and 2 in the specification field direct the machine to compute only the mean (1) and standard deviation (2), even though other statistical options are available.

Within the specification field, the most extensively used symbols are TO, THRU, BY, WITH, EQ, and LT. The words TO and THRU direct the computer to view the connecting statements as inclusive, as in V1 TO V10 or V11 THRU V20. BY and WITH charge the system to compute certain desired relationships. By way of illustration, placing a BY in the specification field of a CROSSTABS procedure card (e.g., V1 BY V2) directs the computer to run a cross-tabulation program using the two variables. A WITH expression is used with the Pearson's product-moment correlation and regression-analysis programs. The remaining two alphabetic symbols are used primarily in variable transformation. EQ stands for "equal to", and LT for "less than".

Each SPSS program has a corresponding procedure card containing a unique command keyword in the control field along with exclusive orders in the specification field. CROSSTABS, for instance, is the control command keyword that directs the computer to execute cross-tabulation procedures. The following is a list of the most frequently used control expressions in the SPSS repertoire:

FREQUENCIES: one-way frequency distributions and measures of central tendency for nominal data

CONDESCRIPTIVE: one-way frequency distribution and measures of central tendency for metric data

CROSSTABS: cross-tabulation procedures and computations of certain nonparametric statistics

PEARSON CORR: zero order or product-moment correlation coefficients for normally distributed metric data

NONPAR CORR: Spearman or Kendall rank-order coefficients

PARTIAL CORR: linear relationships between two or more variables while adjusting for the effects of additional variables

REGRESSION: standard or stepwise regression analysis

FACTOR: factor analysis designed to reduce a large number of variables to a smaller set of valid dimensions

DATA TRANSFORMATION Generally speaking, data are seldom used in the form in which they are originally coded and stored because each researcher usually wants to manipulate them in his own way. Then, too, an important informal coding rule states that more data codes should be used than will be needed, since categories can be combined or collapsed easily. (For coding, see Appendix B.) For these and other reasons, not the least of which is manageability, data are often (though not necessarily) modified before statistical functions are enacted. Such transformations only alter data temporarily. Of the many data modification programs in the SPSS arsenal, the two most extensively employed are data selection and file modification.

Data selection. While data selection includes more than the SELECT IF procedure, that is by far the most frequently applied. The control keyword SELECT IF enables the researcher to choose a unique set of cases in which he has particular interest. As an illustration, assume that the researcher is interested only in the opinions of those respondents who have at least attended college. The coded question, referred to as V6, with its answers is:[3]

(V6)

HOW MANY GRADES OF SCHOOL DID YOU FINISH?

(IF LESS THAN 12) DO YOU HAVE A HIGH SCHOOL EQUIVALENCY DIPLOMA OR CERTIFICATE?

HAVE YOU HAD ANY OTHER SCHOOLING? (WHAT WAS THAT?)

11. 1 GRADE OR LESS: NONE

12. 2 GRADES

13. 3 GRADES

14. 4 GRADES

15. 5 GRADES

16. 6 GRADES

17. 7 GRADES

18. COMPLETED 7 GRADES OR LESS PLUS NON-COLLEGE TRAINING

21. 8 GRADES

22. COMPLETED 8 GRADES PLUS NON-COLLEGE TRAINING

31. 9 GRADES

32. 10 GRADES

33. 11 GRADES

41. 9 GRADES PLUS NON-COLLEGE TRAINING

42. 10 GRADES PLUS NON-COLLEGE TRAINING

43. 11 GRADES PLUS NON-COLLEGE TRAINING

50. EQUIVALENCY [PRIORITY OVER CODES 11-43]

51. 12 GRADES: COMPLETED HIGH SCHOOL

61. 12 GRADES PLUS NON-COLLEGE TRAINING

71. SOME COLLEGE OR JUNIOR COLLEGE

81. BACHELOR'S DEGREE

(UNDERGRADUATE STUDY) BS, BA, AB, AB in TH, B ARCH, B CH E, BCL, BCS, BE, B ED, BFA, BJ, B Lit, BSA, BSC, BSED, BSFS, BS IN CE, BS in CHE, BS in FD, BS in LS, JCA, LITR, PHB, SB, STB, BD

---

[3]Adapted from Inter-University Consortium for Political Research, *1972 American National Election Research* (Ann Arbor, Michigan: Inter-University Consortium for Political Research, 1973).

82. MASTER'S DEGREE MS, MSC, MA MAT, MBA, BDS, MED, MFA, EDM, LLM, MPH, MPA, MS in LS, MSW, MUSM, SM, STM, MMUS, MFS, MSLS

83. PHD, LITD, SCD, DFA, DLIT, JSD, SJD, DPH, DPHIL.

84. LLB, JD

85. MD, DDS, DVM, VS, DSC, DO (DOCTOR OF OSTEOPATHY)

86. JCD, STD, THD

87. HONORARY DEGREE LLD, DD, LHD

98. DK

99. NA

To select only those respondents who attended college, the data selection card would read:

```
1                        16
SELECT IF                (V6 GT 70 AND V6 LT 87)
```

As a result of the above programming expression, only those respondents with at least some college experience would be utilized in any of the remaining manipulative and statistical functions conducted by the researcher.

File modification. When the user is not satisfied with the existing coding format, he may conveniently recode any or all of the variables in a file. To accomplish this, the keyword RECODE is punched in the card's control field. Then, specific recoding instructions are placed in the specification field. If, for the sake of illustration, the investigator wishes to rearrange and/or collapse the values of the previously mentioned education variable, V6, the data will be modified accordingly:

```
1                        16
RECODE                   V6 (11 THRU 22=1) (31 THRU 61=2)
                         (71 THRU 81=3) (82 THRU 87=4)
                         (ELSE=9)
```

CROSS-TABULATION PROCEDURES Probably the most far-ranging program in the SPSS manipulative and statistical arsenal is that of cross-tabulation procedures which enable investigators to compute bivariate joint frequency distributions with one or more independent variables. Simply put, CROSSTABS generates a variety of percentages, nominal and ordinal correlation coefficients, and significance tests. For the beginner the most useful output produced by CROSSTABS is percentage tables. Yet percentages, as valuable as they are, yield only a limited amount of analytical information. Consequently, a complementary STATISTICS card allows researchers to request a variegated number of statistics, among which are chi square, phi, Kendall's taus, and gamma.

CROSSTABS. The cross-tabulation operation most extensively employed by researchers is CROSSTABS. To activate this function, the keyword CROSSTABS is punched in the control field. The specification field, in the meantime, contains a variety of commands, usually connected by keywords such as TO, BY, and THRU. The essential specification command used to direct the cross-tabulation program is BY. Variables in the specification field to the left of BY are row variables (usually dependent), whereas variables to the right of the *first* BY are column variables (normally independent). Lists of variables for either rows or columns can be referenced merely by utilizing the inclusive specification keyword TO. Thus, the command V1 TO V3 BY V9 directs the computer to output three tables. It is equivalent to asking for V1 BY V9, V2 BY V9, and V3 BY V9. Conversely, another similar command could order the computer to output tables with various column (independent) variables. The statement would read V1 BY V1O TO V2O.

Moreover, the SPSS program permits the user to ask for more than one group of tables with a single control keyword by separating each requested table with a slash (/) or a comma (,). The following illustration indicates some of the many ways in which the CROSSTABS procedure card can be punched:

```
V1 BY V2
V1 BY V2, V3
V1, V10 BY V20
V1 BY V2/V2 BY V3
V1 TO V10 BY V20
V1 BY V10 TO V20
```

All these examples represent tables having one dependent variable and one independent variable. The investigator also can ask for a table with more than a single column (independent) variable. To request such a table, the user merely adds another BY and follows it with the second column variable (e.g., V1 BY V2 BY V3). For each additional column (independent) variable desired, just add a BY followed by the appropriate variable. A simple CROSSTABS procedure card is:

```
1                       16
CROSSTABS               TABLES=V1 BY V3 BY V4/V3 BY V4
```

OPTIONS and STATISTICS. The options card, which permits a person to choose particular computations from a variety of functions, contains the command OPTIONS in the control field. In the specification field the user selects either the numbers representing available functions or the word ALL, if all of the functions are chosen. The most frequently requested functions available with CROSSTABS are:

1. Missing values are included in the requested table
2. Variable and value labels are not printed
3. Row percentages are deleted from the output
4. Column percentages are deleted from the output
5. Cell percentages are deleted from the output

An example of the options card is:

```
1                       16
OPTIONS                 1, 3, 5
or
OPTIONS                 ALL
```

In the first instance, the computer would produce only those functions associated with options 1, 3, and 5. In the second, all functions in the CROSSTABS program, including those not listed here, would be run by the machine. When the researcher does not want any functions, this card can be physically deleted from the SPSS setup.

The statistics card is like the options card in that the former allows the user to select one or more statistical options from those already programmed into the SPSS system. Some of the prepared statistics are:

1. Chi-square—Fisher's exact test for 2×2 tables with N less than 21; Yate's corrected chi-square on 2×2 tables with N greater than 21
2. Phi for 2×2 tables and Cramer's V for larger tables
3. Contingency coefficient
4. Lambda
5. Uncertainty coefficient
6. Kendall's tau b
7. Kendall's tau c
8. Gamma

The statistics card substantially resembles the options card. A representation of the statistics card is:

1	16
STATISTICS	1,4,5

or

STATISTICS	ALL

Like the options card, the statistics card can be eliminated if none of the prepared subprograms are desired.

The following statements represent simple RECODE and CROSSTABS procedures by which data stored on a disk can be readily accessed.

DEC format

```
$JOB FACTUR ¢1212,12! /TIME:00:10:00/UNIQUE:1
$PASSWORD PLUM
$DECK JEH.SPS
RUN NAME             VGNDA
GET FILE             NAT. SPS
RECODE               V13 (11 THRU 22=1) (31 THRU 61=2)
                     (71 THRU 81=3) (82 THRU 87=4)
                     (ELSE=9)
CROSSTABS            TABLES=V12 BY V13 BY V15
OPTIONS              3,5
STATISTICS           1,8
FINISH
$EOD
$TOPS10
.RUN SPSS¢5,5!
DSK.LF=JEH.SPS
.Q DSK.LF/DI:D
$EOJ
```

IBM format.

```
//1212,12,'HY',TIME=10
//      EXEC PGM=SPSS
//GO.FT03F001 DD VOL=SER=240136,DSN=FIVNA, UNIT =DISK
//    DISP=(OLD,KEEP),DCB=(LRECL=80,BLKSIZE=1600,RECFM=FB)
//GO.SYSIN DD*
RUN NAME             VGNDA
GET FILE             FIVNA
RECODE               V13 (11 THRU 22=1) (31 THRU 61=2)
                     (71 THRU 81=3) (82 THRU 87=4)
                     (ELSE=9)
CROSSTABS            TABLES=V12 BY V13 BY V15
OPTIONS              3,5
STATISTICS           ALL
FINISH
/*
```

The part of this chapter dealing with specific SPSS setups, it should be remembered, is not designed as a substitute for the SPSS manual. It has attempted to describe some of the programs and functions novices find beneficial and to utilize illustrations pertaining to both DEC and IBM computers. The user, therefore, is urged strongly to *consult the SPSS manual frequently* after he has become acquainted with this elementary presentation of the system. In addition to programs presented in this chapter, SPSS contains an invaluable list of error messages as well as a summary of computational formulae. Moreover, SPSS allows the user much more programming latitude than described in this succinct essay.

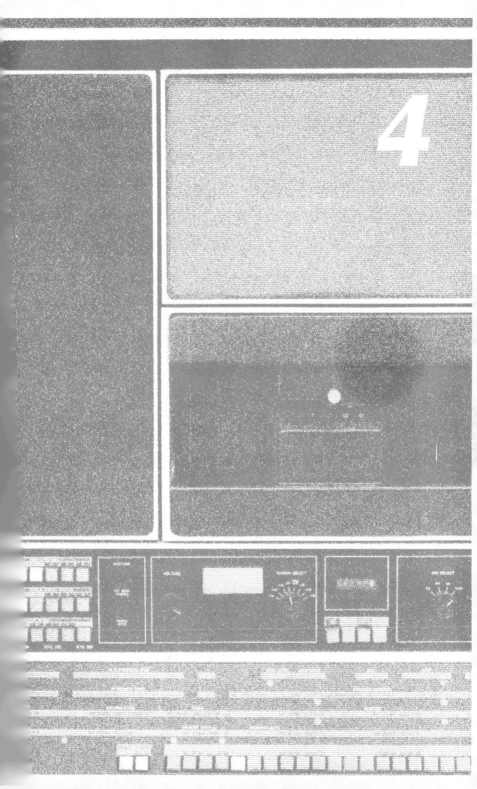

Writing A Quantitative
Research Report

The most carefully designed exploration is of little value unless the findings are communicated to others. The best way to disseminate a study's findings to a large number of persons is by means of a written report.[1] Communication through the written word, however, is a rather arduous task, since a variety of concentrated material has to be presented with precision, lucidity, and clarity, the essential components of good literary form. Any type of writing, whether technical or creative, is a complex process involving art, skill, and a set of grammatical rules. The correct use of grammar is as much an integral part of the research process as is the ability to handle a computer. After all, few researchers can transmit their findings in a clear and logical manner with bad grammar. But good writing consists of more than proper grammar; it involves organizing thoughts and developing ideas. That is to say, writing requires tools somewhat different from those discussed earlier in this book.

Although this is not the place to explain rules of writing, a summary of writing tips is shown in the following checklist:

CHECKLIST #1

1. Organize the material
2. Use specific language
3. Use transitional phrases
4. Avoid unneeded words
5. Shun unnecessary repetition
6. Define terms and concepts precisely
7. Rewrite and edit the report assiduously

---

[1]To be precise, a *report* is a poignant and brief account of some specially investigated matter. A report is not to be equated with a *research article*, which, by contrast, is a fully documented and complete analytical examination, grounded in a solid theoretical foundation.

This chapter describes a research report instead of a research article because there frequently is no need to write an article similar to those which appear in major journals. Besides, some academic journals, particularly in psychology and sociology, require short reports. Furthermore, the researcher working for a business or governmental agency is likely to be asked to limit his report to a few printed pages. Thus one must be selective about what is presented in the report. In a short report, discussion of the theoretical foundations of the study is omitted, except for reference to summaries in the portion of the report that describes how hypotheses were formulated. Space is also conserved by placing remarks concerning the way concepts are operationalized and the methods and instruments used for data collection in the footnotes rather than in the text of the report.

These cues, hopefully, will aid the neophyte in writing a report without obscuring the main points he wishes to make. (For footnote form, see Appendix C.)

Although several integrated and coherent styles of report writing exist, none can be reduced to a series of mechanical steps, a process the novice might find useful. Having said that, an attempt will be made to describe in some sequential fashion the various components of a quantitative research report. Needless to say, these guidelines should be interpreted with considerable flexibility.

The structure of a well-written research report is schematized in Figure 4.1.

OUTLINING MATERIAL

The process of writing a quantitative research report begins with a preliminary outline. After reading about a topic of interest, the investigator should sketch a project layout which describes the key concepts as well as possible underlying patterns and relationships he expects to find. At this stage, it is useful to diagram on paper a network of possible relationships. Once the chart is completed, it can be re-

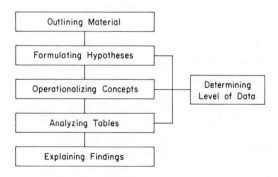

Figure 4.1   Scheme for a research report.

duced parsimoniously to manageable proportions by asking the question: What are the essential concepts in which I am interested?

After the outline is completed, the researcher should compose a working paper which crystallizes thinking and facilitates organization and revision of the final report. A good preliminary paper examines concepts under consideration, prevents key points from being overlooked, and develops a cohesive and integrated method of analysis. Such a paper, it should be emphasized, is simply for the investigator's personal use and therefore can be revised any time he learns more about the topic of interest. Thus, one should never develop a fully detailed working paper at the beginning of a project. The preliminary paper is merely the starting point of a research effort which will be honed into a final report. Its purpose is purely to develop a focus for the research project and report.

FORMULATING HYPOTHESES

Upon completion of a working paper, one or more hypotheses have to be formulated explicitly. Hypothesis development begins with reviewing the findings of others who have studied the same or similar concepts. By exploring the relevant literature concerning particular phenomena, the researcher can familiarize himself with findings, generalizations, methods, achievements, and weaknesses of previous investigations. Moreover, such a review suggests various linkages between concepts and formidable problems associated with the discerned linkages. After the relevant literature has been reviewed, a hypothesis is formulated to coincide with extrapolated generalizations, unless specific reasons exist for developing a hypothesis which runs counter to the reasoning abstracted from previous research.

Hypothesis formulation is the heart of a quantitative research report. Every hypothesis indicates expected relationships among key concepts. The relationship generally is stated in terms of independence and dependence. An independent concept is one that influences (not necessarily causes) another concept, called the dependent concept. Take, for example, the simple hypothesis: *As education increases, church attendance increases.* The independent concept is education and the dependent concept is church attendance. On the basis of previous research and current logic, the researcher determines which concept is independent and which is dependent. A hypothesis then must address two vital questions: What are the essential concepts, and what are the expected relationships between and among them?

Generally, a relational hypothesis is the easiest to conceptualize and understand. A relational association exists when two or more concepts covary. Thus, a relational hypothesis, it should be comprehended clearly, does not deal with causality, because verifying the existence of a relational association does not mean that one concept *causes* another; it merely shows that concepts are associated strongly enough with each other to vary together. Once such interdependent concepts are uncovered, researchers can concentrate their efforts on explaining why concepts are interrelated and speculating on some of the probable sources of causation. Stated another way, if relational analysis demonstrates that two concepts covary, then there is some reason to ruminate about the sources responsible for the association. (Causal relationships also can be hypothesized. But analyzing such associations requires an elaborate research design and sophisticated statistical techniques. Therefore, beginners are encouraged to deal with relational hypotheses, since they can be managed more handily.)

Depending on the level of data available (see the discussion on page 82), a relational hypothesis can be stated in either directional or nondirectional terms. A *nondirectional hypothesis* suggests only that two or more concepts covary; it does not imply the direction in which they covary. (Covariation usually is called a relationship.) An illustration of a nondirectional hypothesis is: *There is a relationship between X and Y.* A *directional hypothesis* stipulates not only that two or more concepts covary but also the direction in which they covary. Moreover, the speculated direction of the hypothesis can be either positive or negative. A positive relationship means that variables vary in the same direction, whereas a negative relationship means that they vary in opposite directions. A directional hypothesis suggesting a positive relationship is: *The more frequently X occurs, the more frequently Y occurs.* A directional hypothesis stipulating a negative relationship is: *The more frequently X occurs, the less frequently Y occurs.*

To help the social scientist, William Goode and Paul Hatt have developed a checklist for drafting relational hypotheses, whether directional or nondirectional.[2] According to them, hypotheses should conform to Checklist #2.

CHECKLIST #2

1. Conceptually clear
2. Empirically verifiable
3. Specific, to the point, and directional (when possible)
4. Related to techniques that are familiar to the researcher

Following these guidelines should help the researcher formulate sound hypotheses.

[2]William J. Goode and Paul K. Hatt, *Methods in Social Research* (NewYork: McGraw-Hill, 1952), pp. 68–73.

OPERATIONALIZING HYPOTHESES

The next step in writing a research report is to operationalize the key concepts used in every hypothesis. Operationalization is a process whereby specific empirical observations, customarily called variables, are used to indicate the existence or nonexistence of whatever is represented by a particular concept. Operationalizing concepts is a complex and difficult task, primarily because there is always a variety of variables that can be used as indicators of any concept. Therefore, when selecting variables to operationalize a concept, one must keep two basic rules in mind. The variable used to measure the concept should (1) fit its commonly accepted meaning and (2) provide the most accurate measurement available.

To insure that these two rules are satisfied, all selected variables must meet the criteria of objectivity, reliability, and validity. Although each of these criteria can be explained in various ways, Frank Scioli and Thomas Cook have cogently and concisely defined each term. The authors state that:

> The requirement of *objectivity* serves to minimize the possibility that the personal bias of the investigator(s) enters into the measurement procedure. The key point is that the results obtained from the measurement procedure should be independent of the particular individual performing the measurement operation. The [criterion], *reliability*, refers to the amount of random error present in the measurement procedure. It is evidenced by the degree of inconsistency of results obtained from repeated applications of a measuring instrument to similar phenomena at different points in time. The greater the inconsistency, the lower the reliability of the measurement, and, therefore, the greater the amount of measurement error present. Closely related to reliability (in a statistical sense) is the question of mea-

surement *validity*. Whereas the above criteria are important to a full assessment of a given measurement procedure, the concept of validity is what might be called the "acid test" for any measurement operation. A measurement procedure may...be fully objective in providing guidelines for reproduction of the measures, highly consistent in repeated application (i.e., reliable); but if the resultant measures are not validated indicators of the decision-relevant concepts contained in the study, they are suspect—suspect in the sense that they may be irrelevant to the analytical question(s) posed in the study.[3]

Even though all criteria should be fulfilled when selecting a variable as an indicator of a concept, the most essential is validity, because it serves as the foundation. In other words, if a variable is a valid indicator of a concept, that variable probably can meet the other criteria. If, however, a variable is not a valid indicator, then no matter how reliable or objective that variable is, it will be an unacceptable indicator of a concept.

There, to be sure, are various ways in which the validity of each selected variable is verified. Whenever a variable is established solidly in the language and culture of a society as an indicator of a concept, the variable has *face validity*.[4] Personal income is understood by most persons to be an indicator, though incomplete, of economic well-being. When a variable is considered to be a valid indicator by a restricted reference group (e.g., economists), it has *convention validity*. Per-capita income is a valid indicator which has convention validity. Finally, when a variable strongly correlates statistically with other variables having face or convention validity, it has *correlational validity*.

[3]This excerpt from "Impact Analysis in Public Policy Reserach," by T.J. Cook and F.P. Scioli, Jr., is reprinted from *Public Policy Evaluation*, Vol. 2, p. 101 (K.M. Dolbeare, ed.). © 1975 by Sage Publications, Inc. Reprinted by permission of publisher and authors.

[4]The following is extrapolated from Ronald W. Johnson, "Research Objectives for Policy Analysis", in Dolbeare, p. 87.

For beginners, the best way to make sure that variables meet the criteria of operationalization is to use the same variables other researchers used when they operationalized similar concepts, rather than try to experiment with original and creative operational definitions. Checklist #3 shows criteria for dependable operationalization.

CHECKLIST #3
1. Objectivity
2. Reliability
3. Validity

One technique that allows the novice to operationalize a concept accurately is to form an index of several variables to measure the extent of its validity. The principal reason for employing an index of variables is that the investigator must, as nearly as possible, exhaust the operational definition of a concept. Needless to say, there is more than one conceivable definition for any concept. Thus, no single variable can operationally account for every possible facet of a concept. By using several variables, the researcher can be confident that all or most aspects of a concept are measured.

Assume, for a moment, that the concept being analyzed is health care. One variable that can be used as an indicator of health care is the number of practicing physicians. If the number of physicians increases over time, it could be concluded that the health-care system has improved. But a person would be on safer methodological ground if an index composed of several variables were used to verify the improvement of the health-care system. For example, one might use an index composed of the number of dentists, the number of nurses, the number of deaths, the number of births, the number of hospital facilities, and the number of extended-care facilities as well as the number of physicians.

The important point to be made from this discussion of concept operationalization is that only when researchers intersubjectively select reliable and valid indicators will a variable be specific, explicit, and precise enough to verify a concept. Furthermore, regardless of the level of data used, it is essential to note that few productive analyses are conducted with invalid and unreliable variables.

DETERMINING THE LEVEL OF DATA

Before developing a hypothesis and operationalizing concepts, one must recognize the level of data with which he will be working, because the data dictate the type of hypothesis that can be formulated as well as the kind of statistics that can be used. The level of data is determined by the level of measurement applied to variables selected to indicate a concept. In the social sciences, three levels of data are generally used—nominal, ordinal, and metric.

Nominal data, considered to be the lowest level, are merely grouped information consisting of two or more categories. (Sex, for example, has two possible categories—male and female.) There is no attempt to determine whether one category is better, stronger, or more desirable than another. The categories, which are based on a combination of common usage, logic, and convention, must be both mutually exclusive and exhaustive. Categories are exclusive when they do not overlap, thus assuring that each observation can be assigned to one and only one category. Categories are exhaustive when they include all possible classifications. (See Coding Conventions in Appendix B.)

Once categories are established, numerical values can be assigned to them. When, for instance, a respondent is classified by sex, a numerical value of 1 can be given if the person is male and of 2 if a female. (Since numbers are assigned arbitrarily, it matters little whether males are given a 1 or a

2. Males could be assigned a 5 and females a 3.) The assigned number merely represents the possession of a categorized property. Therefore, about the only quantitative function that can be performed with nominal data is counting the number and percentage of observations that fall into each category.

Ordinal data are more powerful than nominal data, because the former provide additional information about the property being examined. Ordinal data are categorized properties that are ranked according to some explicit or implicit scale. In other words, ordinal data are comparative assessments of a given property. Besides knowing whether a property holds, the investigator can ascertain an array of variations for each existing attribute. For instance, ordinal data indicate not only whether a respondent likes or dislikes Arthur Wiesczeczinski, but also the degree to which that person likes or dislikes Arthur (e.g., strongly likes, likes, neutral, dislikes, or strongly dislikes). In other words, ordinal data allow the researcher to rank the degree of a particular property in the rather imprecise terms of "greater than" or "less than".[5] Ordinal data are often imprecise in that the interval between two responses such as "strongly likes" and "likes" cannot be measured exactly. But, even though the precise differences among categories are unknown, the property variations still can be ranked comparatively. Thus, ordinal data are more powerful than nominal data, because the former not only indicate the prevalence of categorical properties but also allow such properties to be ranked.

Metric data constitute the most powerful level. They include both *interval* and *ratio data*. (For a definition of these

---

[5]Convention does not suggest how numbers should be assigned to properties, except that the numbers should be in order, since they represent the ranking of the measured property (e.g., 1 = strongly likes, 2 = likes, 3 = neutral, 4 = dislikes, 5 = strongly dislikes).

terms, see the Glossary.) But in social-science research almost all interval data also qualify as ratio data.[6] As a result, the same statistics can be applied to both types. Therefore, for the convenience of the beginning researcher both are incorporated under the term metric. If the exact interval between two or more units is known and a zero indicates the absence of a measurable property, then data are *ratio*. Income is ratio data because the interval between $1000 and $1500 is known to be $500 and zero represents the absence of an income. If the interval between two or more units is known and the zero point is fixed arbitrarily, then data are *interval*. Fahrenheit temperature is interval data, since the distance between 35° and 40° is known to be 5°, but 0° is arbitrary because it does not indicate an absence of heat or cold.

The primary difference between metric and ordinal data is that the former are founded on a more precise scale. An ordinal scale does not permit one to measure the exact number of units between and among categories. For instance, the difference between "strongly agree" and "agree" cannot be measured precisely because it varies among respondents. Some will feel that strongly means adamantly agree, while others will think that it means mildly agree. Thus, a person can never know the precise difference between categories. Metric data, on the other hand, allow one to measure precisely the units of difference between and among categories. The difference between 40 percent and 50 percent is exactly and always 10 percent.

The point of this discussion is that, as previously mentioned, the level of data sets guidelines for the type of hypothesis which can be formulated and the kind of statistics that can be employed. Using nominal data limits the re-

[6]E. Terrence Jones, *Conducting Political Research* (New York: Harper and Row, 1971), p. 32.

searcher to stating *nondirectional hypotheses*, since such data can only indicate the strength of a relationship; that is, the extent of the presence or absence of a given property (e.g., in terms of frequency of occurrence).

Unless data are scaled according to some explicit or implicit criterion (which nominal data are not), direction cannot be inferred. If, for instance, the possible responses to a question about religious affiliation are "Protestant", "Catholic", and "Jewish", a person could hardly say that a Catholic is more (or less) Jewish than a Protestant. Thus to talk about direction when using nominal data is meaningless. The one exception is that dichotomous nominal data can be treated as ordinal or metric data because it is inherently scaled. For example, if the possible responses to a question about a person's race are either "black" or "white", one can conclude that the more white a respondent is the less black he is (and vice versa). Since more or less statements can be made, talking about direction makes some sense.

Ordinal and metric data permit one to develop *directional* hypotheses, since such data, because they are capable of being scaled, can measure not only the strength of a relationship but also the direction of that association. Consequently, when using ordinal or metric data, a more specific hypothesis can be generated and investigated.

In addition to establishing guidelines for formulating a hypothesis, the level of data dictates the kind of relational statistics that can be employed when assessing the extent to which two or more concepts are related. Besides scrutinizing frequencies of occurrence, normally in the form of percentages, researchers can utilize a variety of other statistics which reflect—in the form of correlation coefficients—the strength and, in appropriate instances, direction of relational associations. Since nominal data, considered to be the simplest form of quantitative information, are limited to elementry mathematical operations, only statistics which calculate the strength of a relationship can be applied to test a nondirectional hypothesis.[7] Ordinal and metric data are more powerful than nominal data, because these two types of data are ranked according to some explicit or implicit scale. This attribute means that slightly more sophisticated statistics which measure the strength and direction of an association are applicable and will permit a directional hypothesis to be checked.[8]

At this point, five caveats pertaining to ascertaining levels of data are enumerated in Checklist #4.[9]

CHECKLIST #4

1. Grouped metric data are treated as ordinal data.
2. Metric data frequently are created from nominal and ordinal data by using percentage-of-occurrence figures (e.g., percentage of blacks in Iowa).
3. Dichotomous data, even when nominal, may be used as either ordinal or metric data.
4. The type of hypothesis and statistic is determined by the lowest level of data being used. For instance, when one concept is measured nominally and another concept metrically, the data usually are treated nominally. If one concept is measured ordinally and the other metrically, the data usually are treated ordinally.
5. Hypotheses should be formulated and statistics applied to the highest level of data being used. For example, whenever ordinal data are used, one should not state a nondirectional hypothesis or use a nominal statistic.

---

[7]Some of the most widely used statistics of association for nominal data are phi, lambda, Tschuprow's T, Cramer's V, and Goodman and Kruskal's tau. See G. David Garson, *Handbook of Political Science Methods* (Boston: Holbrook Press, 1971), pp. 155–158; Jones, pp. 111–116.

Familiarity with the items in Checklist #4 is crucial because these items affect the way data are manipulated and analyzed.

ANALYZING TABLES

After discussion of hypothesis formulation and concept operationalization, the reader is presented for inspection and interpretation a summary of quantitative results, usually in tabular form. Such a table should always be presented in a fashion that makes it easily understood without having to refer to the text of the report. Also, each table must be numbered so that it can be identified quickly. Although styles vary, the simplest way to number tables is consecutively with either Arabic or Roman numerals. Then, too, a table should have a title which reminds the reader of the hypothesis. When a brief title is used, the dependent concept is listed first, followed by the independent concept or concepts; for example, "Vote by Income and Education". A more complex title, on the other hand, would describe succinctly the expected relationship.

Furthermore, the table layout should reflect the hypothesis. Convention dictates that the independent concept (or concepts) is placed at the top of the table, and the dependent concept at the left-hand side. Moreover, whenever the hypothesis is directional, the key cell should

---

[8]Some of the most popular statistics of association for ordinal data are Kendall's taus, Goodman and Kruskal's gamma, and Somer's d. For metric data the most prominent statistics are Pearson's product-moment correlation, partial correlations, and regression analysis. See Garson, pp. 170–199; Jones, pp. 116–132, 146–156.

[9]It is beyond the scope of this book to discuss the complex mathematical reasons why data are handled as mentioned within this paragraph. If the student does not have a background in statistics, the instructor will have to help him, or he may read any comprehensive statistics book.

be in the upper left-hand corner of the table, because tabular relational statistics are calculated on diagonals. (When the hypothesis is nondirectional, the position of the key cell is not important, although the independent concept still should be put at the top and the dependent concept at the left-hand side of the table.)

If a directional hypothesis speculates a positive relationship (e.g., *The more frequently X occurs, the more frequently Y occurs*), the table should look like this:

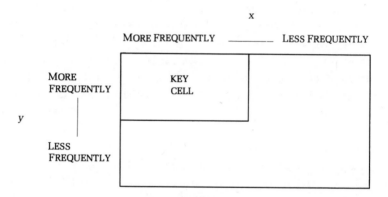

If a directional hypothesis suggests a negative relationship (e.g., *The more frequently X occurs, the less frequently Y occurs*), the table should look like this:

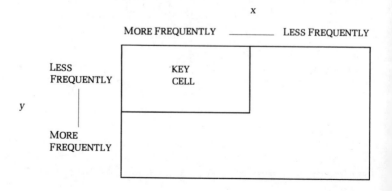

Because of the nature of correlational statistics, such a table layout assures the researcher of a positive correlation coefficient when the hypothesis is substantiated and a negative one when the hypothesis is negated, regardless of the direction of the hypothesis.

An equally important comment pertaining to tabular analysis is that statements should always be made in terms of concepts, not numbers. Put differently, write in English, not in numerics. Beginners have a tendency to cite number after number. Too often the analysis of a table is written like this: "Fifty-five percent of the people who have a high income attend church often. Forty-five percent of the people who have a medium income attend church often. Thirty-five percent of the people who have a low income attend church often." Statements like this go on *ad infinitum*. Instead, one should simply state that as people's incomes increase, they are more likely to attend church.

For illustrative purposes, the following directional hypothesis, involving two independent concepts (education and income) and one dependent concept (church attendance), is cross-tabulated in Table 4.1. Notice that when more than one independent concept is used, the table must be subdivided into partial relationships. (Recall that a directional hypothesis requires ordinal data, which in turn demands ordinal statistics.)

HYPOTHESIS: As education and income increase, church attendance increases.

The data are presented in Table 4.1. The steps in the analysis are as follows: First and foremost, the correlation coefficients should be described in relation to the hypothesis. More specifically, the coefficient shows what relationship, if any, exists between income and church attendance in each of the educational categories. The interpretation of the statistic (in this case T_b) is most easily accomplished by

TABLE 4.1   Percentage of Church attendance by education and income

Church Attendance	High Education			Medium Education			Low Education		
	Income			Income			Income		
	H	M	L	H	M	L	H	M	L
Often	62.5	45.5	18.8	51.9	53.8	19.5	59.1	38.3	26.0
Sometimes	37.5	51.5	51.9	48.1	36.5	55.3	36.4	50.8	50.4
Never	0.0	3.0	29.3	0.0	9.6	25.2	4.5	10.9	23.6
$N=$	8	33	133	27	52	123	44	128	369
	$T_b = .327$			$T_b = .335$			$T_b = .208$		

looking at the strength and direction of the correlation coefficient, located at the bottom of the table. The strength and direction of the coefficient will indicate whether the hypothesis is substantiated or negated. (When using nominal data, a nondirectional hypothesis, and nominal statistics, one should look only at the strength of the association because the direction is meaningless.)

Those unfamiliar with statistics should note that a correlation coefficient is a number that indicates the relationship between two or more variables. An ordinal statistic shows both the strength and direction of that relationship. The values of the coefficient run from -1 to $+1$. The nearer to either end of this scale the coefficient is, the stronger the relationship. Whenever the statistic is positive, the independent variable (concept) and the dependent variable (concept) vary in the same direction. When, however, the coefficient is negative, the variables (concepts) vary in opposite directions. For instance, if the relationship between education and annual income resulted in a positive correlation, the investigator could say that as educational attainment increases, so does income. On the other hand, if the same relationship produced a negative correlation, the researcher could conclude that as educational attainment increases, income decreases. A correlation coefficient of zero indicates that there is no relationship between the variables (concepts).

By looking at Table 4.1, one can conclude that a person's income is related positively to his church attendance because all three of the correlation coefficients are at least moderately strong and positive. Moreover, a person's level of education affects this relationship. The effect of education on the primary relationship between income and church attendance can be determined first by observing the coefficients for each subtable. If the coefficients for each of the three subtables had been virtually identical, one could have said that education has no effect on the primary relationship. However, since the correlations for each subtable are somewhat different, the investigator can assume that education has some impact on the primary relationship. When the second concept, in this case education, does influence the primary relationship, the next step is to ascertain the direction of that secondary association. In the event that the second concept, education had positively influenced the primary relationship, the strongest correlation would have been among the highest-educated group and weakest among the lowest-educated group. Conversely, if education had negatively influenced the primary relationship, the strongest correlation would have been among the lowest-educated and the weakest among the highest-educated. But since the strongest correlation is found among persons who have a medium level of education, it can only be reasoned that education also influences a person's church attendance, though not in either a positive or negative direction.

Besides explaining correlation coefficients, the percentage figures within the table can be interpreted. At this point, a brief comment about computing percentages is in order. It is common practice to calculate percentages in the direction of the independent concept because on the basis of prior research and logic the researcher generally is interested in the consequence that the independent concept has on the dependent concept; otherwise, he would have transposed the two concepts. When, as previously suggested, the independent concept is placed at the top of the table, percentages are tallied by column. (Columns run vertically and rows run horizontally.)

Whenever analyzing percentages, the investigator should discuss general trends and not engage in a cell-by-cell examination of the data. That is, do not mention the numbers one by one. After all, the reason percentages are investigated is to provide the analysis with more detailed information than can be furnished by coefficients and not to confuse and bore the reader. The best way to analyze relational associations among hypothesized concepts with percentages is to inspect and discuss the factors highlighted in the fifth checklist.

CHECKLIST #5

1. Cells having the greatest range of percentage variations
2. Overall pattern, if determinable
3. Inconsistencies and abnormalities
4. Reliability of the total N

The elements in the checklist are examined simply by making comparisons within and across columns. After analyzing the table by examining percentage as well as correlational data, the investigator is ready to speculate on *why* concepts are related the way they are.

EXPLAINING FINDINGS

To expound upon the findings, a person must look beyond a table's percentage figures and correlation coefficients to ascertain why each hypothesis is substantiated or negated.[10] Such an exercise is the least mechanical and therefore most difficult and challenging. There are, however, a few basic guidelines that can make the explanatory process less awesome. For instance, the way in

[10]In the process of determining why a hypothesis is substantiated or negated, one may discover new relationships. Therefore, while an original hypothesis provides a fundamental reference point, subsequent developments, whenever important, should be incorporated into the report.

which concepts are operationalized has to be evaluated carefully, especially when a logically derived and well-researched hypothesis is negated. Such an assessment is accomplished simply by answering a few crucial questions. Were data collected at different times? For example, data in the investigator's table may have been gathered in 1976, whereas the reviewed studies may have used data that were collected in 1964. Were data categorized differently? If one author grouped education into "grade school", "junior high", "high school", "college", and "postbaccalaureate", his findings may differ from those of the researcher who collapsed education into "grade school", "high school", and "college". Were the questions different from those used by other authors? The query, "What is your family income category", for instance, differs significantly from "What was your personal income for the past year?" Then, too, the hypothesis may have been incongruent with the area being analyzed. Although Democrats tend to be "liberal" nationally, they may be quite "conservative" in specific areas of the country. While the aforementioned questions are not an all-inclusive list, they indicate the types of initial queries that should be made when analyzing the results of an empirical investigation.

Claire Selltiz and her coworkers have listed three other aspects on which the researcher should focus after analyzing the tables. According to these writers, any explanation of the findings should include:

1. A statement of the inferences drawn from the findings in this particular situation which may be expected to apply in similar circumstances. The inferences may be at a level quite close to the data or may involve considerable abstraction. For example, in [a] group-leadership example, if the investigator has found more satisfaction, better attendance, more participation, and higher grades in groups that elected their own leaders, the investigator may simply conclude that in

similar situations, election of the discussion leader will have similar effects. However, the investigator may wish to carry this inference to some higher level of abstraction, especially if there is some partially developed theory to which findings may be linked, or if there have been other studies in which the specific phenomena are different but can be understood in terms of the same abstract principle. Thus, for example, the investigator may treat election of the group leader as an example of the more abstract concept *autonomy*.

2. As a qualification of these inferences, investigators should note conditions of their studies that limit the extent of legitimate generalization. They should, for example, remind the reader of the characteristics of their samples and the possibility that they differ from larger populations to which one might want to generalize; of specific characteristics of their methods that might have influenced the outcome; of any other factors they are aware of that might have operated to produce atypical results.

3. Finally, the discussion of implications of the findings will usually include relevant questions that are still unanswered or new questions raised by the study, perhaps with suggestions for the kinds of research that would help to answer them.[11]

Stated simply, an attempt must be made to analyze the findings as they relate to the hypothesis. In other words, why was the hypothesis substantiated or negated, and why did the concepts relate to each other the way they did? In order to explain these questions, the investigator must speculate about the larger consequences of a relationship by linking his findings to those of scholars who have probed similar relationships and to other knowledge about the subject matter (e.g., examining a whole set of ideas about what influences the dependent concept).

[11]Claire Selltiz et al., *Research Methods in Social Relations* (3rd ed., New York: Holt, Rinehart and Winston, 1976), p. 505. Reprinted by permission of publisher.

The final part of a research report should briefly summarize the principal findings of the project as they relate to each developed hypothesis, as well as speculate why these relationships occurred. (Even though speculation, imagination, and creativity are desirable when analyzing the findings, such activity should never be undisciplined and undirected.) Of course, the investigator must be cautioned not to attach exaggerated importance to the findings. One can prevent this situation from happening by never allowing generalizations and conclusions to stray from the evidence and always relating the outcomes to existing literature and/or other research projects. Above all, there is no substitute for common sense.

The foregoing discussion concerning the writing of a quantitative report is summarized below:

Summary Of A Preliminary Research Report

1. Formulate the problem precisely. That is, answer the question: "Why are we interested in studying particular phenomena?"
2. Review the relevant literature to "justify" the hypotheses; decide how to manage the problem; and perceive, ahead of time, the methods, achievements, and weaknesses of prior research.
3. Formulate hypotheses explicitly and operationalize the relevant terms.
4. Define methods, techniques, units of analysis, and level of data used in the report.
5. Select statistics that fit the hypothesis and data.
6. Analyze and interpret the tables.
7. Explain the findings. Discuss the negative as well as the positive aspects of the results, methodology, and techniques. State any specific problems that require additional study.

Figure 4.2 shows a rating form which incorporates all the points cited in this chapter. The form is designed to help the beginner analyze his written report.

AUTHOR _____

TITLE _____

	EXCELLENT	GOOD	FAIR	DEFICIENT
Hypothesis formulation				
Operationalization				
Analysis of operationalization				
Table and charts explain text and add to value of article				
Analysis of statistic(s)				
Linking statistic to hypothesis				
Why hypothesis was substantiated or negated				
Article provides information promised in title				
Text is organized in logical sequence				
Clarity and precision of writing				

Figure 4.2   Rating form.

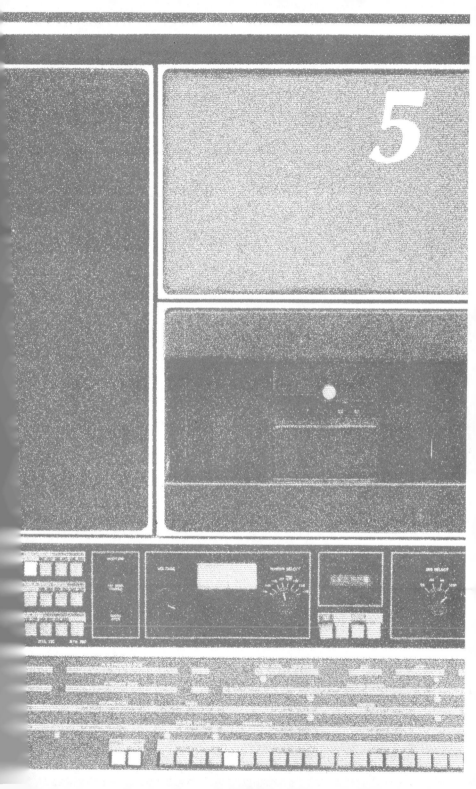

A Final Comment

Now that the beginner comprehends the integral parts of quantitative research—the computer and its components, including prewritten packaged programs, and human judgment—and realizes that such research is not so difficult, he needs to learn more about two essential and widely used research tools, statistical methods and research methodology. Of the two, the novice finds statistical methods, commonly called statistics, the most awesome. The mere mention of the word *statistics* generally drives beginners away, often because they conceive mathematics as a mysterious ritual, rather than as a tool to be used. Because of this natural fear of mathematics, the neophyte must be convinced that statistics is a potent tool for clarifying conceptual thinking and, for that reason alone, is enormously valuable.

Research methodology, for the most part, provokes less vehement reactions, since the beginner is so unfamiliar with the basic building blocks of research strategy that he has no preconceived notions about the subject. One must realize, however, that without some knowledge of research methodology a person is ill prepared to mount any research effort. For example, manipulating and calculating data are simple and straightforward processes compared to developing a research strategy and analyzing and explaining findings. Since such functions are an important part of the research process, one must know about research rules and guidelines, principles commonly taught in research methodology courses.

STATISTICAL METHODS

The term *statistical methods* (or statistics) has a variety of meanings. Some persons define statistics in a concrete sense, such as any set of numbers, averages, or indices. Others define statistics more abstractly. Howard Balsley, for instance, sees statistics as "a system of analysis and synthesis of numerical data for the purpose of obtaining and diffusing knowledge".[1] Most social researchers, however, perceive statistics concretely, since such investigators describe statistics as methods utilized to collect, analyze, and interpret data. Regardless of how statistics is defined, it inherently deals with numbers. Thus, statistics, by its very nature, involves in some form the manipulation of quantitative properties.

The question asked most vehemently and passionately by prospective social researchers is, "Why should I know about

---

[1]Howard L. Balsley, *Quantitative Research Methods for Business and Economics* (New York: Random House, 1970), p. 18.

statistics?" Although there are varied and complex answers to this question, two reasons stand out above all others. The most compelling justification is that inasmuch as quantitative research is devoted to analyzing and verifying objectively relationships among concepts, the investigator needs tools to help him perform these functions. This need, as Ralph Kolstoe indicates, requires social researchers to rely increasingly on mathematics for data analysis because it permits one, by formal means, to examine various relationships in a relatively simple manner.[2]

For the social researcher, the most useful mathematical tool is statistics, since it is oriented toward distilling information from a large amount of quantifiable data and drawing logical conclusions from that information. Statistical logic is a powerful instrument which helps an investigator express ideas (usually in symbolic form) about various relationships and deduce generalizations for restricted situations. More specifically, Edward Tufte suggests that statistics enables the researcher to accomplish five distinct, though interrelated, operations. These are as follows:

Test theories and explanations by confronting them with empirical evidence

Summarize a large body of data into a small collection of typical values

Confirm that relationships in the data did not arise merely because of happenstance or random error

Discover some new relationship in the data

Inform readers about what is going on in the data[3]

[2]Ralph H. Kolstoe, *Introduction to Statistics for the Behavioral Sciences* (Homewood, Ill.: Dorsey, 1973), p. 1.

[3]Edward R. Tufte, *Data Analysis for Politics and Policy* (Englewood Cliffs, N.J.: Prentice-Hall, 1974), p. 1. Reprinted by permission of publisher.

Statistics, then, should be perceived as a mathematical tool to be used to see if substantive generalizations which are formulated on the basis of both logical deduction and previous evidence are either substantiated or negated.

The other principal reason for knowing about statistics is simply that with such knowledge one can read intelligently social science reports, articles, and books. Authors who write articles, reports, and books which examine and transmit knowledge pertaining to social research rely, in varying degrees, on statistical methods. Thus, a person needs to know statistics if he is to understand what he is reading. In addition, authors can misuse and misapply statistics. Such abuses usually are the result of ignorance rather than intention. To cite an example, factor analysis is a popular and powerful statistical technique used in social research. The method, however, requires metric (interval or ratio) data. Yet, it is not unusual to find persons employing factor analysis to ordinal or nondichotomous nominal data. Without some preparation in statistics, one might accept this sort of statistical sleight of hand as legitimate, when, in fact, it is not. A person can only protect himself against such blunders by becoming statistically literate, meaning that at the very least he should know how, where, and when to apply appropriate statistics as well as how to interpret them.

The prospective social investigator should become familiar with two families of statistics, *descriptive statistics* and *inferential statistics*. Descriptive statistics simply summarize mass observations in a manner that makes data more understandable and manageable than they were in their original form. Such statistics are quite useful because the social researcher frequently is confronted with considerable amounts of information, and to make some sense of it, he needs some technique for describing it concisely. Suppose for a moment that after interviewing 2000 respondents an investigator wants to know whether the males and females differed in their opinions about professional football. The easiest way to discover whether differences exist is to use a descriptive statistic such as a percentage. One could compare the percentage of males favoring professional football with the percentage of females favoring it. Thus, the 2000 observations can be summarized by two simple descriptive statistics.

The other type of statistics with which a person should become familiar is inferential statistics, which are used to make inferences about an entire population of which an investigator has information about only a part. At this juncture, one needs to understand two key statistical concepts—*population* and *sample*. The term *population* refers to all members of any group being studied—for instance, Polish-Americans, or states of the United States. A *sample*, on the other hand, is a subset of a population. (A sample frequently is used in quantitative analysis, since it often is impractical to examine an entire population.) The use of inferential statistics, then, involves mathematical techniques based on probability of occurrence, which allow the researcher to presume (through inference) that the descriptive characteristics found in an analyzed sample are not unlike those existing in the population.

To see the utility of inferential statistics, one needs only to look at the way in which pollsters know how 150 million Americans feel about a particular matter. These social technologists certainly cannot interview every person in the country. Instead, they randomly sample the opinions of approximately 1500 persons. When the sample of individuals is chosen according to rigid statistical requirements, the selected persons may be assumed to represent a cross section of inhabitants. As a result, the technologist can infer, within a range of probability, that the expressions of the sample respondents represent the population's opinions.

More specifically, inferential statistics allows the investigator to ascertain exactly how similar the sample is to the population, so that he will know what degree of confidence to place in each inference.

These two types of statistics, descriptive and inferential, are enormously powerful tools that can be used to facilitate the organization and interpretation of quantitative information by providing answers to some crucial questions: What is the central tendency of the data? How much variation is there? Do the concepts correlate? How large should the sample be? Is the sample similar to the population? Is the hypothesis substantiated or negated?

RESEARCH METHODOLOGY

Besides becoming statistically literate, anyone who is interested in understanding and conducting quantitative research should know something about research methodology. Although there are a variety of ways to define methodology, it is best described as the study of how to examine logically hypothesis formulations, research designs (e.g., experimental, nonexperimental, descriptive, explanatory, causal, and relational), measurement tactics, data collection methods, and analytical techniques, as well as slightly more abstract aspects of research such as theory construction and ethical and value questions. This inventory of topics suggests that methodology is a complicated set of skills that helps a person conduct research with greater precision.

Why should a beginner spend time acquiring methodological skills? To be sure, there are varied and complex reasons, but some are more apparent than are others. The most obvious benefit is that methodological knowledge complements computer and statistical skills. In other words, knowing how to manipulate the computer and apply and interpret statistics is of limited utility unless one understands the logic behind the research process. A person, therefore, must know how to identify logical fallacies, engage in the inductive-deductive reasoning cycle, formulate and test hypotheses, and develop a set of interrelated generalizations from the results of an empirical investigation.

Understanding the methodological aspects of empirical research helps one appreciate the necessity of integrating analytical methods with substantive knowledge. An investigator has to realize that any quantitative examination of social phenomena depends upon his thoroughly knowing the subject. Qualitative research is a concomitant part of any quantitative examination. When data are analyzed without the benefit of a qualitative exploration of the subject under consideration, there is a grave danger that the entire research project will be misconceptualized.

Furthermore, methodology contributes to a person's ability to evaluate the research efforts of others. Stated more explicitly, an understanding of methodological rules and quidelines allows one to ascertain the amount of confidence he can place in another researcher's findings. To cite an example, a person's confidence in someone else's results is increased when that researcher does not succumb to the following pitfalls:

1. Inaccurate observations
2. Selective observations
3. Illogical reasoning
4. Premature closure of inquiry
5. Overgeneralization.[4]

Methodology also familiarizes a person with various steps in the analytical process.[5] For instance, the inves-

[4]Earl R. Babbie, *The Practice of Social Research* (Belmont, Ca.: Wadsworth, 1975), pp. 14–18.

[5]David Nachmias and Chava Nachmias, *Research Methods in the Social Sciences* (New York: St. Martin's, 1976), pp. 8–9.

tigator should be able to *recognize concept covariation.* Two concepts are said to covary when a change in one concept is associated with a change in another concept. Take, for example, the finding: *As a person's income increases, his job security increases.* The concepts income and job security vary together; if they do not covary, one concept remains unchanged while the other varies.

Next, a person should be able to *eliminate spurious relationships.* Such an association takes place when one concept appears to affect another concept but is actually influenced by a third unknown or untested concept. The finding: *The more policemen the city employs, the higher its rate of crime,* if interpreted causally, is a spurious relationship, since policemen do not create more crime. There are other factors—such as the size of the city's population—that cause crime and also affect the number of policemen employed by the municipality.

Then, too, a researcher should be concerned with *establishing order of occurrence.* The time element probably is the investigator's most important reference point for dealing with causal relationships. Obviously, X cannot influence Y, if Y happens before X. To take an absurd yet clear example, there is no way the assassination of President John F. Kennedy could have been a cause of World War II, because the assassination happened after, not before, the war. However, when X can be shown clearly to have occured before Y, the researcher can deduce that X *may have* caused Y. It is possible, therefore, that the election of President Lyndon B. Johnson influenced United States participation in the Vietnam conflict, since the election happened before the event.

Finally (although this is not an all-inclusive list), the prospective social science researcher should be able to *develop an interrelated set of empirical generalizations,* often referred to as theory. Such generalizations are developed for the purpose of suggesting why phenomena behave the way they do, thus helping the researcher explain the importance of his observations. Sets of empirical generalizations also should be linked to other theories about the same or similar phenomena so that the study being conducted can support or refute the established theories. In this way, the investigator transcends the role of a technician and becomes a scientist.

To grasp fully the utilities, limitations, distortions, and problems of quantitative research, a person must learn how to analyze reality. Such an analysis requires a set of skills that helps one think systematically about the complexities of empirical research. Methodology is such a skill, which when properly applied can aid in the examination of the underlying assumptions and the logic of the methods used to develop a group of interrelated generalizations and which, consequently, is as integral a part of the quantitative research process as is statistics.

Coupled with an understanding of statistical methods, research methodology is an integral tool which facilitates the organization, interpretation, and explanation of quantitatively measured phenomena, Methodology, then, is a cumulative effort that establishes guidelines to inform the social investigator of past mistakes so they can be avoided in the future. With these insights a researcher can increase the power of his quantitative analysis, thus enhancing the value of the research effort.

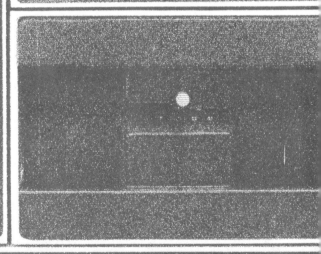

Appendices

Appendix A
Card Punching

After data are collected and coded, they normally are translated into a language that the computer can recognize. Since the digital computer cannot read handwritten data, such information has to be transformed into electronic impulses so that the machine can understand it. To do this, the researcher generally punches the coded data together with appropriate instructions onto computer cards via a key-punching machine. Then, these cards are read into the computer and stored on either core or auxiliary storage units.

The most widely used computer card is made by International Business Machines (IBM). (IBM's closest competitor is Remington Rand. Its card has a different layout from IBM's, but translating machines can read cards punched in one system and convert their impulses into the other.) Physically speaking, the standard IBM computer card is 7⅜ inches long, 3¼ inches wide and 0.007 inch thick. Since the card is divided into 80 horizontal columns and 12 vertical rows, there are 960 possible positions where data can be punched. Normally, one hole is punched in each column to record numeric data, whereas a combination of two or more holes per column records alphabetic data.

The two topmost rows on each card are reserved strictly for alphabetic information, the third row is for 0's, the fourth is for 1's, and so forth. The number 6, for instance, is punched in row nine. Although the preceding information is not useless, it is not necessary for the researcher to know the exact hole location that corresponds to each character, since most keypunching machines print the punched character on the top edge of each card.

Each computer card moves, column by column, from the hopper to the punching station. After it is punched it is automatically released to the reading station. From there the card moves to the stacker. This process continues until all data and instructions are recorded on punched cards, whereupon they are transmitted to the computer. Figures A.1 and A.2 show a keypunching machine and a keyboard for such a machine.

The data punched on the computer card are read by the computer as cards are fed seperately through a machine called a card reader. This device automatically converts the presence or absence of holes into electronic impulses.

The following instructions are designed to help the neophyte card puncher operate the IBM 029 keypunching machine.

INSTRUCTIONS FOR THE USE OF THE IBM 029 KEYPUNCH[1]

1. *Place cards in hopper.* Place unused cards in the feed hopper located at the right top part of the machine.

Push the pressure plate back until it stays back, and place the cards in the hopper with the 9 edge (bottom edge) down, and with the front of the cards toward you. Gently release (by squeezing the bar) the pressure plate, which will spring against your cards, placing them flush against the front of the hopper, ready to be fed into the machine.

2. *Turn keypunch on.* If necessary, turn the keypunch on. The main line switch is located under the keyboard near your right knee. "On" is up. When you sit down at a keypunch you will often find that it is already on.

3. *Release program control level. Check the program unit to see if the small star wheels are lifted off the surface of the cylinder. If they are not, push the right side of the switch (located underneath and to the left of the program unit) in to raise the wheels.*

4. *Keyboard switches up.* Flip up all the functional control switches (above the keyboard) with the exception of the CLEAR switch, which stays down. If there is an INTERPRET/PUNCH switch on the far left of this row of switches, move it to the PUNCH position.

5. *Push the* FEED *key.* This key (right side of the keyboard, second row from the top) causes a card to be fed from the card hopper into the punching bed, putting it into the preregistering position.

6. *Push the* FEED *key again.* This causes another card to be fed from the card hopper into the punching bed, and at the same time registers the first card for punching at the punching station. *Note:* If you want to punch only one card, push the REG key at this step. This has the effect of registering the first card without feeding a second card into the punching bed.

7. *Keyboard information.* Keypunch the desired information onto the card using the appropriate keys. Hold

[1]Source: *Reference Manual IBM 029 Card Punch.* Reprinted by permission. © International Business Machines Corporation.

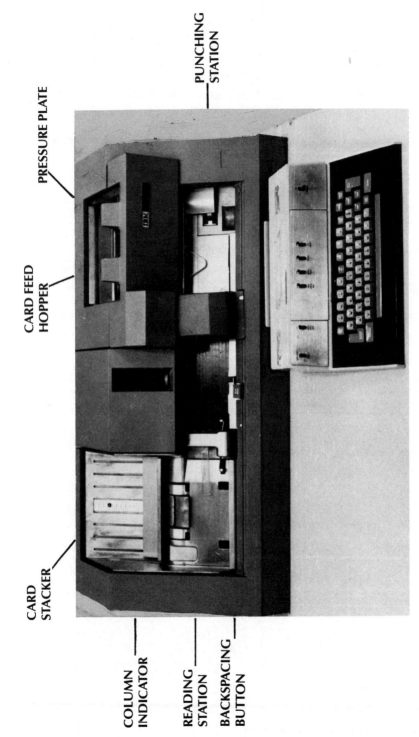

Figure A.1 Keypunch. [COURTESY OF INTERNATIONAL BUSINESS MACHINES CORPORATION]

Figure A.2 Keyboard for a keypunch. [Courtesy of International Business Machines Corporation]

down the NUMERIC key only for characters shown on the upper half of the keys. Push the space bar each time a column is to be left blank. *Note*: (a) Backspacing is accomplished by pushing the button at the center of the card punch. The card will continue to move backwards as long as the button is held down. You cannot correct a mistake by backspacing it to a column and punching the correct character over the incorrect one. This will only make extra holes in the same column, creating a new combination of holes which is meaningless. (b) The column indicator, which can be seen through the window of the program unit, indicates the number of the column which is currently in position at either the reading or the punching station. The column indicator will be particularly useful when you are correcting cards with punching errors. Notice that only the even-numbered columns are identified and that the odd-numbered columns have the long marks.

8. *Release card.* Push the REL key when you have finished punching a card. This causes four things to happen: (a) if the card is at the reading station, it moves up into the card stacker; (b) the card at the punching station moves into the reading bed and is registered at the reading station; (c) the card in preregistering position in the punching bed is registered into the punching station; (d) another card is fed from the card hopper into the preregistering position of the punching bed.

9. *Clear machine.* When you have completed your punching, lift the switch marked CLEAR on the face of the keyboard. This will move the cards in the track through to the card stacker without feeding new cards from the card hopper, thus clearing the track. The CLEAR switch springs to the down position as soon as you release it.

10. *Using the* DUP *key to your advantage.* The DUP (dupli-
cate) key is used for correcting errors. Depressing it
causes the information in the card at the reading station to be duplicated in the corresponding column of
the card at the punching station. Thus, if you discover
an error in only a few of the punched columns, you
may use the DUP key to avoid keypunching the entire
card again. For example, suppose you discover that
columns 61–62 (and no others) of a card have been
mispunched. The original card should be positioned
in the reading bed and a blank card in the punching
bed. (In this context, it is useful to note that cards may
be inserted into the empty reading and punching beds
directly, without first being inserted into the card
hopper.) After both cards have been properly registered, the first 60 columns may be duplicated by depressing the DUP key. It is necessary to look at the column indicator to determine when the 61st column is
in position at the punching station. The next two columns can now be corrected by punching the correct
characters in the usual fashion. The remaining columns can be duplicated by again pressing the DUP
key.

11. *Card jams.* If your keypunch jams a card, do not try to
pull it out from under the punching station or reading
station by hand. Seek help from a computer-center
worker who knows how to clear a jam. Improper
technique in getting the card out can badly damage the
keypunch.

Appendix B

Coding Data

To understand further how large quantities of data are manipulated by the computer, a person must be familiar with some elementary coding procedures, since the digital electronic computer can only manipulate information that has been transformed into symbols which in turn are transformed into electronic impulses. In quantitative research, numbers usually are assigned to measured properties because numerals are handled with greater ease by the machine than are letters or other characters (e.g., +, −, /, *). This process of converting properties to symbols is called *coding*. In other words, a number is allotted to each property of each variable of each case. (A case is the smallest recorded thing whose attributes are being observed. Simply put, a case is an observed unit. It can be, for example, an

121

individual, county, state, or country.) All data for each case are recorded on one or more computer cards by punching an assigned number which corresponds to the existence of a given property in the appropriate column or columns. Thus, coding is a procedure by which an investigator constructs a classification scheme that translates a variable's attributes into numeric symbols, which are representations of real-world phenomena.

With nominal data, for instance, the respondent's sex can be recorded in column 3 by punching a 1 for male or a 2 for female. Ordinal data can be transcribed by punching a 1 in column 4 if the respondent "strongly agrees", 2 if he "agrees", and so forth. For metric data, actual integers can be placed in the appropriate columns. When a person answering a questionnaire is 92 years old and the variable, age, is recorded in columns 5 and 6, a 9 is then punched in column 5 and a 2 in column 6. (Directions for using keypunching machines are in Appendix A.)

CODING DESIGNS

Social-science data, whether nominal, ordinal, or metric, are collected predominantly from two principal sources: surveys and statistical records. Surveying involves eliciting answers from respondents to predesigned sets of questions, whereas statistical records are data gathered by private or public agencies, usually in aggregate form. Survey techniques concentrate on gathering information about the respondent's social traits, attitudes and opinions, and political knowledge and behavior. Such inquiries utilize either closed-ended, open-ended, or rank-listed questions.

Closed-ended questions offer the respondent highly structured alternatives. Frequently, alternative answers to questions involve three to five possible choices, such as "strongly agree", "agree", "no opinion", "disagree", and "strongly disagree".

Open-ended questions, on the other hand, have no structured alternative answers. In essence, they are essay questions. For instance, a question could read, "Which organizations would you say are the most influential in state politics?" The respondent can reply to the question in any manner he chooses.

Rank-listed questions are used primarily to determine respondents' priorities. Customarily, they list alternatives, which they then ask each respondent to rank according to some criterion. A question might read: "Which of the following four candidates do you feel is best qualified to be governor of this state? List them in order from best to worst." The answer might be, "J. B. Bristol, L. Y. Myers, A. K. Lilly, and O. P. Bayer".[1]

Most closed-ended and rank-listed responses are easily coded by simply assigning numbers to each alternative answer and punching the appropriate integers in specific columns (e.g., strongly agree = 1, agree = 2). On the other hand, the unstructured open-ended responses pose certain difficulties. Since written answers cannot be manipulated and calculated readily by most computers, it is necessary to develop manageable categories from the unstructured responses. If the question reads: "What is your occupation?", the researcher has to construct categories such as "highly skilled", "skilled", and "unskilled" from the myriad written responses in order to make sense of the variegated replies.

Besides survey responses, another type of easily coded data, popular among social scientists, comprises statistical records. Enormous quantities of such data are gathered by private, public, and quasipublic agencies. Among those most frequently used are census material, state and local

[1]There are advantages and disadvantages associated with each type of question: see C. H. Backstrom and G. D. Hursh, Survey Research (Chicago: Northwestern University Press, 1963), Chapters 3 and 4; and Earl Babbie, Survey Research Methods, (Belmont, Cal.: Wadsworth, 1973), Chapter 10.

data, election returns, congressional and legislative information, and a variety of other comparative statistics. In annotated bibliographies, several authors have listed the locations of all types of private and public information.[2] Material gathered from statistical records is coded in the same manner as are answers to survey questions; that is, data are regarded as open-ended, closed-ended, or rank-listed, whichever is most appropriate.

CODING CONVENTIONS

There is a variety of formal and informal coding rules and regulations, and some of them are exceedingly important to remember. The eight most crucial are:

1. The number of categories should be sufficient to allow a variation of responses or observations. To be on the safe side, the coder should develop more categories than are needed, since they can always be collapsed later.
2. The researcher should use as many values per variable as needed. When coding the variable "political-party identification", the coder may be tempted to list the values as "Democratic", "Republican", "other", and "no response". It might be wise to classify the category "other" into at least "independent" and "Socialist" in case the researcher eventually decides to conduct a more detailed analysis of political-party identification than was originally intended. Combining categories is much easier than recoding after the initial coding has been performed.

[2]R. L. Merritt and G. J. Pyszka, *The Student Political Scientist's Handbook* (Cambridge, Mass: Schenkman, 1969); Carl Kalvelage et al., *Research Guide for Undergraduates in Political Science* (Morristown, N.J.: General Learning Press, 1972); and E. Terrence Jones, *Conducting Political Research* (New York: Harper and Roe, 1971).

3. The range of categories for each variable should be all-inclusive, so that all responses or observations can be assigned to some category. Caution should be exerted to see that categories do not overlap, thus assuring that each observation can be assigned to one and only one category. Moreover, any coding scheme must provide for all possible answers, including responses such as "no response", "don't know", and "not ascertainable".

4. Generally speaking, blanks should not be used when coding data, inasmuch as the lack of a punched hole in any column of the computer card can raise doubts as to whether the researcher merely failed to punch an integer in that particular column. Therefore, always assign an integer (zero, if there is no number to be punched) to each column.

5. A consistent coding scheme should be employed. If, for example, alternative responses for a number of attitudinal statements in an ordinal closed-ended questionnaire are "agree", "no opinion", and "disagree", all like replies should be assigned the same integer to avoid confusion and aid the analyst.

6. The coding scheme, whenever possible, should correspond to actual values of the data. When the variable is ordinal in form, the highest number should be assigned to the most positive answer, the lowest to the most negative. When the variable is grouped annual income, for instance, and its values consist of categories such as "less than $7500", "7501–$10,000", and "more than $10,000", an annual income in the first category would be coded 1, and one in the third category would be coded 3. An income of approximately $8000 would be coded 2.

7. Although the coding scheme should be tailored to requirements of the analysis, the researcher is advised to maintain detailed, logical, and consistent patterns

when translating qualitative answers into machine language. Convention further suggests that categories be exhaustive and mutually exclusive because many packaged statistical programs will not process multiple-punched variables (data which have more than one answer per category). Generally multiple-punched responses are not used as frequently as they were in the past because, as Earl Babbie states:

Multiple punching and the use of blanks are both part of the legacy of an earlier era in survey analysis when researchers were limited to a single IBM card (80 columns) per respondent. Today, most researchers have access to computer programs that permit the use of many cards per case.[3]

When more than one answer per response or observation is desired, each possible answer should be treated as a separate reply.

8. There is no natural scheme for coding nominal data.

[3]Babbie, p. 194.

Appendix C

Footnote Form

Footnotes are essential to scholarly writing. Using properly, they allow important information to be communicated to the reader without detracting from the logical development of the text. Footnotes customarily are used not only to disclose bibliographic citations, indicating the source of a quotation or idea, but they also permit researchers to discuss interesting sidelights which, though informative, are somewhat peripheral or explanatory to parts of the text.

The two most frequently asked questions about footnoting are: (1) When do I use a footnote? and (2) What form of footnoting should I use? Although volumes have been written about footnoting procedures, there unfortunately appears to be no clear answer to the first question. A careful review of the literature shows that, generally speaking, footnotes should be used whenever the researcher directly quotes an author, summarizes someone else's discussion, arguments, or opinions, or attempts to explain or otherwise add facts pertinent, but external, to the report. The answer to the second question concerning style is relatively straightforward. Although the form varies, footnotes are placed either at the end of the report or the bottom of each page of the text. In front of each footnote is a reference number (often raised one-half space) which corresponds to the one placed in the text immediately following the documented statement. The footnote usually is single-spaced with a double space between each one and the next. (The first line of the citation is indented five typed spaces.) The succeding footnote models normally are sufficient for most citations used in a quantitative report. When specific problems are encountered, consult one of the many manuals available.

GENERAL FORM

Books

[1]Thomas R. Dye, *Politics in States and Communities* (Englewood Cliffs, New Jersey: Prentice-Hall, 1973), pp. 1–5.

Periodicals

[2]Lawrence C. Dodd, "Committee Integration in the Senate: A Comparative Analysis", *Journal of Politics*, 34 (November 1973), 1137.

Newspapers

[3]*The New York Times*, May 18, 1974.

ABBREVIATIONS

References already cited in detail may be written in a brief form:

[4]Dye, pp. 108–120.

If more than one book by the same author is utilized, the second citation of one of the previously cited books would appear with the author's last name, the title, and page number:

[5]Dye, *Politics, Economics and the Public Policy Outcomes in American States*, p. 5.

Ibid., meaning "in the same place" is used to cite a work for the second time immediately after it has been referenced in the previous footnote:

[6]*Ibid.* (Means same title and same pages.)

[7]*Ibid.*, pp. 102–103. (Means same title, different pages.)

SPECIAL PROBLEMS

Two Authors

[8]Thad Beyle and J. Oliver Williams, *The American Governor in Behavioral Perspective* (New York: Harper and Row Publishers, 1972), p. 67.

More Than Two Authors

[9]William A. Rosenbaum et al., *Analyzing American Politics* (Belmont, California: Wadsworth Publishing Company, Inc., 1971), p. 4.

Edited Work

[10]Allan P. Sindler, ed., *Policy and Politics in America: Six Case Studies* (Boston: Little, Brown and Company, 1973), p. 56.

Explanatory Footnote

This type of citation is used to add explanation or amplification of a particular point under discussion. The information usually given is extraneous to the material presented in the body of the paper, and, if included, would divert the reader from the main points being presented in the text:

[11]The size of a computer's memory system usually is measured in K bytes, which are units of 1,024 bytes. Thus a computer with a core capacity of 128 K has 131,072 bytes of memory.

Glossary

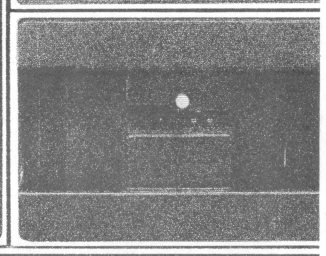

Basic Glossary of
Data Processing Terms

Alphabetic A term pertaining to a set of symbols consisting of the letters A–Z.

Alphanumeric A term pertaining to a set of symbols containing letters (A–Z) and numerical digits (0–9).

Analog computer A machine that performs manipulative and statistical operations using physically measurable variables such as length, width, and voltage.

Arithmetic-logic unit A part of the computer performing mathematical and logical operations.

Auxiliary storage The computer's memory device that is not directly accessible to the central processing unit (CPU). Such a device expands and augments a computer's storage capacity.

Batch processing A mode of computer programming that requires the user to assemble a group of instructions and process them sequentially. The user cannot interact with the programs once they begin to run.

Binary data system Numerical information based on powers of 2, that is, the numbering system contains only two digits—usually 0 and 1.

Bivariate A term pertaining to statistical analysis involving two variables.

Bug A mistake in a program or user setup.

Byte The storage needed for one character. Storage capacity is often measured in bytes.

Card A 3¾ × 7⅜ inch "Hollerith" or "IBM" card for punching information, containing 12 rows and 80 columns.

Card punch A device used to record information on cards by making holes in the cards to represent letters, digits, and special characters; also called a keypunch.

Card reader A mechanism which senses the holes punched in a computer card and transforms that information into a form with which the computer can deal—electronic impulses.

Case The information obtained from a single unit (e.g., person, state) of a sample or population.

Cathode-ray tube (CRT) A device allowing the user to communicate with the computer. The output is displayed on a mechanism similar to a television screen.

Causal hypothesis A speculated relationship suggesting that an independent concept is associated strongly enough with the dependent concept to cause it to vary.

Cell A compartment at the intersection of a row and a column.

Central processing unit (CPU) A part of the computing system including the circuits that perform the requested manipulations and calculations.

Character A letter, digit, or other symbol used to represent data, to control operations, or to organize; a blank is also considered a character.

Character printer An output device that prints visual records on paper one character at a time.

Code A system of rules and symbols representing data or operations. Loosely, any of the characters resulting from the use of a code.

Codebook A book containing variable titles, code ranges, and code meanings.

Coding A process by which information obtained from a study is reduced to a set of numeric or alphanumeric (mnemonic or nonnumeric) values suitable for input into an analysis procedure.

Collapse The process of reducing a number of categories to fewer categories.

Column A distinct vertical array for representation of characters: a vertical series of cells.

Column total The total of the value counts (percentage, frequency) in one vertical series of cells.

Column width The number of characters in a field.

Compute directions Coded commands instructing the computer to execute a logical or arithmetic function.

Computer A machine performing complex mathematical and logical manipulations on the basis of wired or stored instructions; also referred to as Electronic Data Processing machines (EDP). The three most popular types of computers are digital, analog, and special-purpose.

Control statement Preprogrammed commands indicating operational specifications for a program.

Control unit A portion of a digital computer that interprets, initiates, and executes instructions.

Control variable A set of observations whose values define subsets of the data being analyzed. By convention, usually the column variable.

Core storage Magnetic cores (small rings of magnetic material) which function as main storage units. Items in core storage can be located and readied for processing in a few millionths of a second.

Corner total The grand total of value counts (percentage, frequency); the sum of row totals or column totals.

Correlation coefficient (simple) A statistic that shows the degree to which two measurable concepts vary together. The coefficient almost always ranges from +1 to −1. A statistical relationship of +1 indicates that two concepts vary together in the same direction. A relationship of −1 shows that two concepts vary inversely with each other. A relationship of near 0 suggests that two concepts do not vary together.

Covariation A process occurring when a change in one concept is associated with a change in another concept.

Cross-tabulation table A matrix display of the frequencies of data cases among values of two or more variables (e.g., sex according to age group).

Data analysis The process of categorizing or summarizing data for the purpose of drawing inferences, usually employing statistical techniques.

Debug The process of checking input and output from a job in order to find the error in the program.

Deck One of a set of punched cards containing the information for one case. A deck is a single card which is part of a set (e.g., a case for one respondent having three cards would consist of deck 1, deck 2, and deck 3). Loosely, all cards of a file having the same deck number.

Default A procedure executed by a program or the operating system when the user fails to specify a particular option.

Delimiter A symbol that sets apart items of information on a control card. The common delimiters are the blank and the comma. The special delimiters are left and right parentheses and the slash; they are used according to certain rules in specific contexts.

Dependent concept The phenomenon the researcher is trying to explain and/or understand.

Descriptive statistic A mathematical technique used to describe a collection of quantitative data in a convenient and concise form.

Digital computer A computer that performs manipulative and statistical operations using numerically represented information.

Directional hypothesis A suggested relationship that speculates the direction in which independent and dependent concepts covary. A positive relationship speculates that concepts vary in the same direction, while a negative relationship suggests that concepts vary in opposite directions.

Disk A storage device with the ability to directly access a particular file without having to sequentially scan each stored file before reaching the selected file. The magnetic disk is a thin circular plate (much like a phonograph record) coated on both sides with recording material. Disks are mounted on a vertical shaft, slightly separated from one another. As the disk revolves, it is read from or written on by read-write heads mounted on access arms.

Edit The process of examining and/or modifying the representational form and/or format of data for anticipated input and output (stored and/or printed).

Empirical generalization An assumption about the interrelationships among various sets of quantifiable concepts.

Execute card A punched job-control card that designates the program to be accessed and executed.

Field Contiguous columns reserved for a series of characters.

Field width The number of columns reserved for a series of characters.

File An organized collection of information and instructions treated as a single unit for processing.

Format The structure, layout, and method of arrangement of data.

FORTRAN A formula translator system. One of the languages for writing programs. (This is the most common language in which social science programs are written.)

Frequency distribution An array of quantitative data indicating the number of times different values of a variable occur.

General-purpose computer A computer designed to solve a wide range of problems merely by programming the machine to perform the specified tasks.

Hardware Electronic or mechanical equipment used in data processing; physical devices as opposed to programs and methods (software).

Hypothesis A speculated set of relationships between and among concepts. Such associations are based on literature review, experiences, logical deduction and induction, and theoretical formulations.

Independent concept A phenomenon that the researcher thinks will help him explain and/or understand the dependent concept (that which the investigator is trying to explain and/or understand).

Index A composite of several indicators used to measure an independent or dependent concept. Such a set of indicators is used when a concept cannot be measured accurately by a single indicator.

Indicator A variable or combination of variables that is used to determine the existence of a concept.

Inferential statistic A mathematical technique used to determine the amount of risk involved when making a generalization from a sample to a wider population.

Input device A part of the computing system that converts information and instructions into a form that can be understood and used by the computer.

Input instructions A set of commands directing the computer to perform requested functions.

Instructions A set of characters instructing the computer to execute particular operations according to the indicated operands.

Interval data Data categorized in terms of standard units of measurement (e.g., age, years of service) so that the exact distance between units can be determined.

JCL See **job-control language statements.**

Job A series of programs to be executed in a given sequence. Each job must begin with a job card.

Job card A punched card that indicates the beginning of a job and contains accounting information.

Job-control card One of several punched cards indicating programs to be executed, sequence of execution, and requirements for each program.

Job-control language statements The special set of operating instructions used to identify the job, to indicate the necessary programs to be executed, and to locate the relevant data.

Justify A procedure that calls for placing character(s) to the left or right according to a prescribed rule so that the character or string of characters begins or ends in a particular column (e.g., the "word" GET, assigned a field consisting of columns 1–9, would begin in column 1—occupying columns 1, 2, 3—if left-justified, and would end in column 9—occupying columns 7, 8, 9—if right-justified).

Keypunch A device used to record information on cards by making holes in the cards to represent letters, digits, and special characters.

Keypunching The manual punching of information on computer cards.

Keyword command A statement that retrieves prewritten and stored statistical and manipulative program(s) so that they can perform requested functions.

Line printer An output device that prints visual records on paper one line at a time.

Logic A process by which a person subjects a series of propositions to the principles and criteria of validity.

Machine readable A term pertaining to preparing information and instructions in a form suitable for input into the computer.

Magnetic disk A widely used auxiliary storage device similar to a phonograph record. (See disk)

Magnetic tape A device much like a recording tape, with a magnetic surface on which data can be stored; a storage medium, read from or written on by a read-write head as the tape moves past the head.

Mark sensing A process by which the computer reads marks made with an ordinary lead pencil, provided the marks are placed in predetermined positions on paper forms or computer cards.

Mathematical model A body of mathematical statements describing processes and parameters and their relationships to each other.

Mean The sum of the scores divided by the total number of cases involved, commonly referred to as the average.

Methodology An examination of the underlying assumptions and logic of the methods used in conducting research.

Metric data Interval and ratio data. Interval data lack a true zero point but have equal intervals. Ratio data have a true zero point and equal intervals. They can be subjected to any arithmetic operation.

Missing data Information that is not present or is deliberately excluded by the user. The data may be absent because certain answers to questions were inappropriate, not ascertained (simply not asked, refused by respondent), or incomprehensible.

Multiple correlation coefficient A statistic that shows the degree to which more than two concepts covary. Like a simple correlation coefficient, it ranges from +1 to −1 and is interpreted the same way.

Multivariate A term pertaining to statistical analysis involving more than two concepts.

Natural language statements Programming commands that use common English.

Nominal data Categorized information having no numerical order. There is no logical basis for performing any arithmetic operations with them, except counting.

Nondirectional hypothesis A speculated relationship suggesting that two or more concepts covary, but failing to stipulate the direction in which they covary.

Numeric A term pertaining to numerals or representation

by numerals. A numeric code includes only digits, 0—9.

Option command A control statement directing the computer to perform specific manipulative and statistical functions. A set of option commands is associated with each keywork command.

Ordinal data Information that can be arranged in less-than and greater-than order but lacks a true zero point and equal intervals.

Output Data that have been processed—stored and/or printed. The device or devices used to take data out of a storage device for printing or external storage.

Output command A set of instructions directing the computer to transfer information to an output device.

Output device A part of the computing system that transforms the information stored in the computer's memory into a form that can be used by the researcher. The most common devices are line and character printers and CRTs.

Parameter Information (characters, numbers, etc.) supplied by the user to select options allowed by a subprogram.

Population A set representing the universe of interest to an investigator.

Prewritten program A master program, designed for general application, that permits the user to retrieve stored operating instructions which direct the computer to perform various manipulative and statistical functions. Thus, it is unnecessary to write detailed instructions every time particular functions are desired.

Printer An output device that takes electronic impulses generated by the computer and prints them on paper in a form that can be understood by the user. There are two major types of printers, character printers and line printers.

Printout A visual, human-readable output printed on paper, in contrast to stored output on cards, tapes, and/or disks.

Problem-solving language A set of numerically and algebraically written expressions permitting the user to communicate with the computer. The two most common problem solving languages are FORTRAN and COBOL.

Program A set of instructions directing the computer to perform basic operations and identifying the data and mechanisms required. The entire series of instructions required to complete a given task. A complete program includes instructions for the transcription of data, coding for the processor, and absorption of results into the system. A program may be unitary or may contain sub-programs, often called routines.

Programming The process by which a set of instructions, arranged in proper sequence, are fed into the computer so it will perform desired operations.

Punched card See **card**.

Range The set of values that a variable may assume (e.g., variable A may assume the range of values 0—9).

Ratio data Interval data that have an absolute zero point representing the total absence of a phenomenon.

Raw data Information prior to input to a computer system. Data which have not been processed or affected in any way by the system.

Read-write heads An assembly allowing the computer to read from or write on auxiliary storage devices.

Recoding The process of changing a character or set of characters to another character or set of characters.

Register A part of the computer in which a subset of information is stored until it is needed to complete the requested arithmetic-logic processes.

Relational hypothesis A speculated relationship suggesting that an independent concept and a dependent concept are associated strongly enough to vary together. There is no attempt to suggest that the independent concept "causes" the dependent concept to vary.

Reproducing Duplicating data in the same medium (cards, tape, disk) as the original with all or part of the information contained in the original.

Row A horizontal series of cells, defined by the value of a row variable (the variable whose values are written vertically at the left side of the table).

Row total The sum of the value counts (percentage, frequency) in one horizontal series of cells.

Run A single, continuous act of processing under the control of one or more programs. All procedures required to produce desired output.

Sample A subset of a population.

Setup The required order of control cards and data in the input deck.

Software Programs, rules, and associated documentation for the operation of a data-processing system (*contrast with* hardware).

Sort The process of arranging units of data in an ordered sequence (ascending or descending).

Special character A symbol other than the letters A–Z and the digits 0–9 (e.g., &, *, −, /, $).

Special-purpose computer A computer designed to solve a limited class of problems. Such a computer is nonprogrammable because it is wired to execute identical operations every time.

Specification commands Prescribed comments telling the computer the exact functions to be performed with specific variables.

Spurious relationship An association occurring when one concept appears to affect another concept but actually is influenced by a third unknown concept.

Statistics Techniques using mathematical operations for collecting, organizing, analyzing, and presenting quantitative data.

Storage unit A device used to store information and instructions so that they may be retrieved when needed. There are two types of storage units, core and auxiliary.

Symbolic language Nonarithmetic symbols that allow the user to communicate with the computer.

Tape mark That part of the tape signifying the end of a file.

Teletype terminal A typewriterlike device allowing the user to communicate directly with the computer.

Time sharing A mode of computer programming permitting the user to interact with a programmed set of instructions while they are being run.

Validity A process designed to determine if an indicator or variable actually measures the concept it is supposed to measure. Three types of validity are face, convention, and correlational.

Value A number or alphanumeric character asssumed by a variable for a particular case.

Variable A specific empirical observation that is given a set of values, usually, but not always, in numeric terms.

Variable list A sequential set of variables whose values constitute the cases in a file. Each variable has a mnemonic; the sequence of mnemonics represents the variable list.

Volume A physical unit of secondary storages (e.g., a reel of tape or a disk pack). Each volume has a serial number used to identify a particular volume containing a data file or a volume which is to contain a new data file.

SOURCE NOTES

"Basic Glossary of Data Processing Terms," in *User's Manual*, II (Computer Services Facility of the Institute for Social Research, University of Michigan).

Norman Nie, Dale Bent, and C. Hadlai Hull, *SPSS: Statistical Package for the Social Sciences*, Appendix E (New York: McGraw-Hill, 1970).

Harold Borko (ed.), *Computer Applications in the Behavioral Sciences* (Englewood Cliffs, N. J.: Prentice-Hall, Inc., 1962).

Eric A. Weiss (ed.), *Computer Usage Fundamentals* (New York: McGraw-Hill Book Company, 1969).

F. R. Crawford, *Introduction to Data Processing* (Englewood Cliffs, N. J.: Prentice-Hall, Inc., 1968).

Selected Bibliography

Chapter 1

BENSON, OLIVER. *Political Science Laboratory*. Columbus, Ohio: Charles E. Merrill, 1969.

BUCHANAN, WILLIAM. *Understanding Political Variables*. New York: Scribner's, 1969.

CAMPBELL, STEPHEN. *Flaws and Fallacies in Statistical Thinking*. Englewood Cliffs, N. J.: Prentice-Hall, 1974.

FITE, HARRY H. *The Computer Challenge to Urban Planners and State Administrators*. Washington: Spartan Books, 1965.

HARKINS, PETER B., ISENHOUR, THOMAS L., and JURS, PETER C. *Introduction to Computer Programming for the Social Sciences.* Boston: Allyn and Bacon, 1973.

HEARLE, EDWARD, and MASON, RAYMOND. *A Data Processing System for State and Local Governments*. Englewood Cliffs, N. J.: Prentice-Hall, 1971.

Chapter 2

ARNOLD, ROBERT R., HILL, HAROLD C., and NICHOLAS, AYLMER V. *Modern Data Processing*. New York: Wiley, 1969.

CRAWFORD, F. R. *Introduction to Data Processing*. Englewood Cliffs, N. J.: Prentice-Hall, 1968.

EMERY, GLYN. *Electronic Data Processing*. New York: Elsevier, North-Holland, 1969.

FARINA, MARIO V. *Computers: A Self Teaching Introduction*. Englewood Cliffs, N.J.: Prentice-Hall, 1969.

FIELDS, CRAIG. *About Computers*. Cambridge, Mass.: Winthrop, 1973.

SAMMET, JEAN E. *Programming Languages: History and Fundamentals*. Englewood Cliffs, N. J.: Prentice-Hall, 1969.

Chapter 3

BENNETT, WILLIAM RALPH. *Computer Applications for Non-Science Students (BASIC)*. Englewood Cliffs, N. J.: Prentice-Hall, 1976.

BLACKMAN, SHELDON, and GOLDSTEIN, KENNETH M. *An Introduction to Data Management in the Behavioral and Social Sciences*. New York: Wiley, 1971.

DIXON, W. J., ed. *BMD Biomedical Computer Programs*. Berkeley: University of California Press, 1967.

INSTITUTE FOR SOCIAL RESEARCH. *OSIRIS III*. Vol. 1: *System and Program Description*. Ann Arbor: The University of Michigan, 1973.

LOHNES, PAUL R., and COOLEY, WILLIAM W. *Introduction to Statistical Procedures: With Computer Exercises*. New York: Wiley, 1968.

NIE, NORMAN H., HULL, C. H., JENKINS, J. G., STEINBRENNER, K., and BENT, D. H. *SPSS: Statistical Package for the Social Sciences* (2nd ed). New York: McGraw-Hill, 1975.

WEIS, ERIC A., ed. *Computer Usage—360 Fortran Programming*. New York: McGraw-Hill, 1969.

Chapter 4

BABBIE, EARL R. *Survey Research Methods*. Belmont, Cal.: Wadsworth, 1973.

BACKSTROM, C. H., and HURSH, G. D. *Survey Research*. Chicago: Northwestern University Press, 1963.

DOLBEARE, KENNETH M., ed. *Public Policy Evaluation*. Beverly Hills: Sage Publications, 1975.

GARSON, G. DAVID. *Handbook of Political Science Methods*. Boston: Holbrook, 1971.

GOODE, WILLIAM J., and HATT, PAUL K. *Methods in Social Research*. New York: McGraw-Hill, 1952.

JONES, E. TERRENCE. *Conducting Political Research*. New York: Harper and Row, 1971.

KALVELAGE, CARL, and SEGAL, MORLEY. *Research Guide in Political Science* (2nd ed). Morristown, N. J.: General Learning Press, 1976.

MERRITT, R. L., and PYSZKA, G. J. *The Student Political Scientist's Handbook*. Cambridge, Mass.: Schenkman Company, 1969.

SELLTIZ, CLAIRE, WRIGHTSMAN, LAWRENCE S., and COOK, STUART W. *Research Methods in Social Relations* (3rd ed). New York: Holt, Rinehart and Winston, 1976.

Chapter 5

BABBIE, EARL R. *The Practice of Social Research*. Belmont, Cal.: Wadsworth, 1975.

BALSLEY, HOWARD L. *Quantitative Research Methods for Business and Economics*. New York: Random House, 1970.

HOOVER, KENNETH R. *The Elements of Social Scientific Thinking*. New York: St. Martin's Press, 1976.

ISAAC, STEPHEN. *Handbook in Research and Evaluation: For Education and the Behavioral Sciences*. San Diego, Cal.: Edits Publishers, 1971.

KOENKER, ROBERT. *Simplified Statistics: For Students in Education and Psychology*. Totowa, N. J.: Littlefield, Adams and Company, 1971.

KOLSTOE, RALPH H. *Introduction to Statistics for the Behavioral Sciences*. Homewood, Ill.: Dorsey, 1973.

McGAW, DICKINSON, and WATSON, GEORGE. *Political and Social Inquiry*. New York: Wiley, 1976.

NACHMEAS, DAVID, and NACHMEAS, CHAVA. *Research Methods in the Social Sciences*. New York: St. Martin's Press, 1976.

PHILLIPS, BERNARD S. *Social Research: Strategy and Tactics* (2nd ed). New York: Macmillan, 1971.

TUFTE, EDWARD R. *Data Analysis for Politics and Policy*. Englewood Cliffs, N. J.: Prentice-Hall, 1974.

INDEX

Prewritten programs (*cont'd*)
 control statements, 46ff,
  135
 functions, 51ff
 (*see also* BMD; OSIRIS;
  SPSS)
Printer, 142
 character, 36
 line, 36ff
Problem-solving language, 38,
  40, 47ff, 143
Programming, 38, 40, 143 (*see
  also* Prewritten pro-
  grams)
Purpose of book, 10ff

Q

Quantification, 102ff, 109

R

Ratio data, 83ff, 143 (*see also*
  Metric data)
Registers, 34, 143
Relational hypothesis. *See* Hypothesis
Relationships
 causal, 77
 negative, 91
 positive, 91
 relational, 77, 144
 spurious, 108, 145
Reliability, 79, 81
Research process
 analyzing tables, 87ff

coding, 121ff, 135
determining data level,
  82ff
explaining findings, 93ff
footnoting, 127ff
formulating hypotheses,
  76ff
operationalizing hypothe-
  sis, 79ff
outlining material, 75ff
sample, 105, 144
writing report, 73, 74ff

S

Selltiz, Claire, 94ff
Special-purpose computer, 18,
  144
Specification field, 60ff
Spurious relationship. *See* Relationships
Statistics, 102ff, 145 (*see also*
  Descriptive statistics; Inferential statistics)
Statistical package. *See* Prewritten programs
Statistical Package for the Social Sciences (SPSS),
  47ff, 60ff
 format, example of, 60ff
 (*see also* Data, modification of; Data, selection
  of; Cross-tabulation procedures)

H
61
.H95

Hy, Ronn J.
    Using the computer
in the social sciences